P9-CZV-115

CHRISTOLOGY BEYOND DOGMA

MATTHEW'S CHRIST IN PROCESS HERMENEUTIC

by

Russell Pregeant

FORTRESS PRESS
Philadelphia, Pennsylvania

SCHOLARS PRESS
Missoula, Montana

Library of Congress Cataloging in Publication Data

Pregeant, Russell.
    Christology beyond dogma.

    (Semeia supplements ; 7)
    Bibliography: p.
    1. Jesus Christ—Person and offices. 2. Bible. N.T.
Matthew—Criticism, interpretation, etc. 3. Bible.
N.T. Matthew—Hermeneutics. 4. Process theology.
I. Title. II. Series.
BT202.P66   226'.2'063   77-78638
ISBN 0-8006-1507-7

6456L77   Printed in the United States of America   1-1507

DEDICATION

Not the "book" (printed word and frozen concept)
But the *process*—call it "work," or "thought," or "agony,"
    or "love"—
That giving-taking-hoping, living-thinking-being
Which in part (but ah, what small a part!) emerges here,
I give to those, first known, through whom Life's values
    first engaged me:

my mother   Eloise White Pregeant
                 (for gentleness of spirit,
                 goodness of heart)

and, in memory,

my father   Victor Eugene Pregeant
                 (for dancing eyes and laughter,
                 and for openness to all)

and my brother   Walter George Pregeant
                 (for courage to live the moment:
                 from childhood's high adventure
                 to life's last, triumphant breath) . . .

O man, how true are thine
instincts, how over-hasty
thine interpretations of
them!
——Matthew Arnold

TABLE OF CONTENTS

Abbreviations 9

Preface 11

PART I: Description and Interpretation:
Toward a New Methodology 15

Chapter 1   The Context of the Present Proposal 19
Chapter 2   Prospectus for a Process Hermeneutic 33

PART II: Outline for an ExperimentalVenture:
Christology and Soteriology in Matthew's
Gospel

Chapter 3 47

PART III: The Components of Matthew's Christology:
Torah, Salvation, Grace 61

Chapter 4   Torah and Salvation: Matt 5:17-20 63
Chapter 5   Torah as Grace: Matt 11:25-30 85

PART IV: The Undercurrent: An Incipient
Universalism 105

Chapter 6   The Explanation of the Parable
of the Tares: Matt 13:36-43 107
Chapter 7   The Description of the Last Judgment:
Matt 25:31-46 115
Chapter 8   A Process Analysis 121

PART V: The Mainstream: A Fragmentary Christology

Chapter 9 129

PART VI: Christology Beyond Dogma:
          The "Catalytic" Christ 143

Chapter 10 Outline for a Critique of
            New Testament Christology 145
Chapter 11 Interpreting the Christ-Image 157
Chapter 12 Excursus 161
Chapter 13 Methodological Implications 165
Chapter 14 Summary 168

Works Consulted 171

ABBREVIATIONS

B	Biblica
CS	The Christian Scholar
ET	Expository Times
HTR	The Harvard Theological Review
Int	Interpretation
JAAR	Journal of the American Academy of Religion
JBL	Journal of Biblical Literature
JR	The Journal of Religion
JThCh	Journal for Theology and the Church
JTS	The Journal of Theological Studies
NRT	Nouvelle Revue Theologique
NTS	New Testament Studies
NovT	Novum Testamentum
PS	Process Studies
PSTJ	Perkins School of Theology Journal
RB	Revue Biblique
ThL	Theologische Literaturzeitung
ThZ	Theologische Zeitschrift
ZNW	Zeitschrift für die neutestamentliche Wissenschaft und die Kunde der älteren Kirche
ZThK	Zeitschrift für Theologie und Kirche

Preface

The possibility of a "process hermeneutic"—a theory of interpretation informed by the understanding of language that undergirds the "process" metaphysics of Alfred North Whitehead—is one that has occurred to a number of persons over the past several years. Conversations on this theme—involving quite a few formal papers—have been taking place at the Center for Process Studies of the School of Theology at Claremont for some time, and a consultation was held at Christian Theological Seminary in Indianapolis in 1974; The Society of Biblical Literature and the American Academy of Religion have sponsored a group on "Process Hermeneutic and Biblical Exegesis" since 1974, and several articles have already appeared in theological journals; two full-length works have, in differing ways, made important contributions: William Beardslee's *A House for Hope* (Westminster, 1972) explores thematic relationships between biblical thought and process conceptuality, and Barry Woodridge's 1976 Claremont dissertation, "The Role of Text and Emergent Possibilities in the Interpretation of Christian Tradition," seeks explicitly to develop a thoroughgoing hermeneutical theory based upon process thought.

The reader familiar with this background will observe, however, that what is presented here stands in relative isolation from much of this previous work. The explanation lies not in any lack of interest in what others have done but in the "redactional" history of the present volume. The first stage was a Vanderbilt dissertation, completed in 1970, in which I sought to evaluate Schubert Ogden's christological perspective, through comparison with that of the gospel of Matthew, as an interpretation of New Testament christology. Although the process components of Ogden's *theology* figured in a minor way in my presentation, and had indeed been a part of my own thought structure for several years, it had not yet occurred to me to make use of a process understanding of *language* as a direct key to the hermeneutical dimension of the problem. That idea came only with my reading of Lyman Lundeen's provocative book on Whitehead's theory of language, *Risk and Rhetoric in Religion*. This encounter led first to a rather sketchy paper, "Toward a Process Hermeneutic," presented to the New England region of the American Academy of Religion in 1973. It was only with the emergence of the "Process Hermeneutic" seminar at the 1974 Annual Meeting of the Society of Biblical Literature, however, that I became aware that I was not alone in my interests. Rather eagerly, then, I prepared a longer piece, "The Matthean Undercurrent," for discussion at the 1975 session. The present volume is a direct outgrowth of that effort. So the approach advocated here is essentially my own, although I believe it can relate positively to, and be enriched by, many of the other attempts to bring process philosophy and biblical studies into conversation.

And the "isolation," I should hasten to add, is indeed relative. For even though I do not wish to saddle anyone else with the specifics of my method, I must acknowledge the crucial roles that some have in fact played in helping me re-think earlier efforts—however much my judgment might still differ from theirs on some points. I profited not only from the formal critiques of "The Matthean Undercurrent" by Ed Everding and Clark Williamson, but also from the comments of David Griffin and David Lull, which sensitized me further to the question of historicity and the richness of Whitehead's notion of "propositions." Important also were a suggestion by Ted Weeden and a glimpse at an early draft of a portion of Barry Woodbridge's dissertation, which combined to heighten my awareness of Whitehead's potential for illumining the "futurity" of a text. And William Beardslee, whose labors have far exceeded the mere "duties" of an editor, has made welcome suggestions regarding both substance and form that have strengthened the final product. that have strengthened the final product.

There are two persons without whose help this work would literally have been impossible: Schubert Ogden, who first introduced me to process thought and has given me encouragement and advice at every stage along the way; and

Leander Keck, whose willingness to work—critically and sympathetically—with an "unorthodox" dissertation set the context for all that has followed. I am also indebted to Curry College for granting me this spring semester's leave in Claremont, which has afforded me the luxury of completing the manuscript with my editor close at hand as well as the opportunity to work more closely with some of those who share my concerns. Particular thanks in this regard must go to Dean Frederick Kirschenmann and my colleague Alan Anderson, who has also provided a stimulus for me through his own creative use of Whiteheadian thought. By the same token, I must also express appreciation to John Cobb and others at the School of Theology and the Center for Process Studies for a warm welcome to Claremont and the prospects of a fruitful stay.

I am indebted to Rosemary Cassels-Brown, of the Episcopal Divinity School in Cambridge, Massachusetts, for assistance in the translation of several German passages. And a word of thanks must also go to the staff of *Process Studies* for permission to reprint material that appeared in an earlier article in that journal (Fall, 1976). Biblical quotations are from the Revised Standard Version of the Bible, copyrighted 1946, 1952© 1971, 1973, and are used by permission of the National Council of the Churches of Christ in the U.S.A.

As my argument in the pages that follow implies, it is the inspiration of certain basic "images" that enables us to determine the quality of our lives and carry out our own particular forms of work and play. The ultimate drive behind this present essay comes from the central images of the New Testament itself: I have pursued them because they do in fact "open up" existence for me. But it is in the concrete lives of human beings that such images are finally interpreted and put to the test. So in listing those who have helped in the making of this book, I must at last mention those whose most significant contributions have been by way of personal inspiration through the years—although each has given me much in more "material" ways also: my "first" family, to whom the book is dedicated; my friend, Tom Matheny, whose activities as a layman in the United Methodist Church give flesh to the image of the missional and inclusive community of faith; and finally and most especially, my wife, Sammie, whose weaving together of joy in living, a sense of the sacred, and sensitivity to the needs of dispossessed humanity is a model and a constant reminder of the real function of all authentically religious speech.

Russell Pregeant
Claremont, California
February 8, 1977

Part I

Description and Interpretation: Toward a New Methodology

If the glory of scientific exegesis is that it has freed biblical interpretation from the grip of supernaturalism and ecclesiastical dictates, its shame is that it has obscured the very nature of the documents it seeks to illumine. For in its attempt to exhibit the meaning of a text in its original setting, this method has in effect presented a dynamic process as if it were a "still."

To abandon the gains of the scientific approach would of course be unthinkable. The tools of literary and historical research are indispensable correlates of the interpreter's intention to let the text speak for itself. But two considerations call into question the adequacy of the scientific model, unaided, to do justice to the text. In the first place, it is simply impossible for any interpreter to view any text with absolute objectivity. The text is in fact unintelligible apart from a point of contact in the interpreter's own experience. Thus it is always appropriated in light of certain questions, values, and perspectives brought to it.

But that is not all! The subtler point is that the text itself *is* interpretation. It is constituted precisely by the reworking of former tradition, whether oral or written, from the vantage point of the writer's life-situation, with the explicit intention of shaping its readers' futures. It is thus by nature only one rather arbitrarily delineated component in an ongoing process. For that reason a hermeneutical method that reveals the text's relationship to its own present and past, but ignores its thrust toward the future, violates that text's very nature to the extent that it implies that the meaning of the work is thereby exhausted.

Descriptive exegesis does, of course, attempt to show how the biblical texts were intended to claim the lives of their original readers. But it overlooks two crucial considerations. What the authors intended can by no means be equated with what their audiences actually heard. These readers had to appropriate the language of the texts in terms of their own situations, not the authors'. Thus even the first reading of a text is creative interpretation and not mere duplication of the author's intention. Beyond that, the modern reader who seeks to understand the meaning of the text for the original readers can imagine the needs, problems, reactions of those readers only by analogy with his or her own life-situation. Thus, commensurate with the actual intention of the text, any description of the original meaning actually becomes—in however small a measure—a link in the ongoing process of tradition.

But there are, unfortunately, varying qualities of tradition. What a merely descriptive exegesis does is to reduce tradition to one dimension and thus obscure the potential of the text to come alive in the interpreter's present in a significant way—not only to merge with that interpreter's world-view but to challenge it, to claim his or her existence, to create a dialogue that goes beyond the level of intellectual apprehension. What is missed is that the text, by virtue of its very nature, has the potential to claim *this* reader also. Thus suddenly to proclaim the process of "contemporization" illegitimate is itself an arbitrary imposition of a modern outlook upon the text, an imposition that reflects a misunderstanding of what that text fundamentally *is*. What is needed is a way of allowing the text to fulfill its own nature by speaking to the world in which the interpreter lives.

The present study proposes an understanding of the nature of language informed by Alfred North Whitehead's process metaphysics as a viable basis for a new hermeneutical method designed to recover the lost dimension of biblical interpretation. My intention is to present the outlines of such a method, as I conceive it, and then to test it by application to a peculiarly difficult problem in New Testament studies. This is the question, raised in one way by Schubert Ogden (1961; see also 1975) and in another way by Herbert Braun, of the "meaning" or "point" of New Testament christology. Before attacking this specific problem, however, I will try to elucidate the approach I envision in terms of its relationship to two other hermeneutical theories also designed to get beyond a merely descriptive methodology: Bultmann's original program of demythologizing, or existential interpretation, and the effort of some of his heirs to achieve a more fully existential reading of the text under the rubric of the "new hermeneutic."

Chapter 1

The Context of the Present Proposal

James M. Robinson (1964) rightly identifies Bultmann's demythologizing project as a specialized instance of his general application of content-criticism *(Sachkritik)* to the New Testament. Basic to this method of interpretation is the view that the language of a given text stands in relative distinction from the basic intention of the text. Stated negatively, this means that language does not exhaust the reality which fosters it and to which it refers. Stated positively, this means that all meaningful language is historically or existentially based.

Bultmann argues that understanding takes place only on the basis of a shared life-experience between author and reader. The human mind does not possess innate ideas to which linguistic symbols may connect themselves. It is only through prior historical experience of a given reality that the signification of that reality has meaning. Texts relating to music, for instance, can speak only to one who has experienced music. Or, more generally, a historical text cannot be understood

> unless you yourself live historically and can therefore understand the life of history, that is, the powers and motives which give content and motion to history as the will to power, the state, laws, etc. (1958:51)

But if language serves understanding by directing one's attention to experienced realities, it is nevertheless always only relatively adequate to the reality it signifies. Hence it is possible to speak of a distinction between what a text intends and what it actually says. The process of balancing the intention disclosed by the language of a text against the entire scope of language used to this end is what Bultmann means by content-criticism. The question which motivates this procedure is whether any given term or frame of reference within a text is appropriate to the primal reality coming to expression.

By applying this method to Paul's discourse on resurrection in I Cor 15, Bultmann discloses a discrepancy in Paul's thought. Although Paul's general usage of the term σῶμα (body) is to indicate a historical, existent self, in this passage the apostle is led by the course of his own argument to use it in the sense of a natural-corporal substance. The result of the shift is that when resurrection is considered, the σῶμα is conceived in terms of nature-analogies and thus loses its quality as a free, responsible agent. The continuity between the historical, existent self and the resurrected body is unwittingly dissolved, and the self's responsibility for its own fate is obscured. In such a case Bultmann does not hesitate to state Paul's intention in distinction from Paul's words and to define the interpreter's task as "to interpret Paul critically . . . to understand him better than he understood himself!" (1964a:63).

Or again, Bultmann shows that Paul often uses terms such as σάρξ (flesh) and πνεῦμα (spirit) in their Gnostic sense—i.e., to refer to substance or power. Such usage in relation to the human self can result only in a deterministic scheme in which that self is the pawn of alien forces which violate its own integrity. So Paul sometimes contradicts his own basic view of the human being—that of an integrated personality responsible for its own future. Thus it is the task of content-criticism to balance the intention disclosed in the whole scope of Pauline language against the meaning contained in certain aspects of that language. And it is the materials themselves, not simply the presuppositions of the interpreter, which provide the warrant for this procedure.

> So we must by all means read Paul critically, and the error of the earlier research is not that it used criticism at all, but that it did so on the basis of a modern world-view, which did not examine its own presuppositions, but proclaimed itself, instead of the intention of the text, as the criterion of criticism. (1964a:262)

Now the programatically developed project of demythologizing is, in Robinson's words, a form of content-criticism "in which the use of mythological language as such is criticized as an objectification, in which worldly categories are simply elongated to express what is actually unworldly" (1964:33). Mythology is inadequate to the New Testament's intention to address humanity because it gives "to the transcendent reality an immanent, this-worldly objectivity" (Bultmann, 1958:19). It reduces God's "qualitative" relationship to the world to "quantitative" terms (Ogden, 1960:18), so that God's actions become phenomena within the world and are perceptible in the same manner as other events. Viewed in this way, both divine and demonic activity necessarily appear as intervention or intrusion into the world. And since the world is invaded by alien forces, the human person is seen as subject to determination by them. Consequently, the person's quality as a decision-making being is obscured. Faith cannot be understood as decision if invested in an objective phenomenon. And human beings cannot really decide their individual fates if they are subject to external domination. The "mistake" inherent in mythological language as used in the New Testament is this: it bases a self-understanding (which is by nature existential, a matter of subjectivity) upon an objective phenomenon (which cannot be existential, since it is a matter of observation).

But it is important to understand that Bultmann does not see demythologizing as the imposition of a modern frame of reference upon the New Testament. His contention is that the New Testament itself clearly presupposes human freedom and unity in its constant use of existential language—language which calls for personal decision. Despite all the mythology, what is finally intended—even by the mythology itself—is the presentation of a human self-understanding before God. This is seen above all in the New Testament's own nascent forms of demythologizing (1961:11f., 19f.). So the real task of exegesis is not to report such information, whether historical or supernatural, as the materials might contain. It is to convey the understanding of human existence that appears in the *address*. Demythologizing is interpreting mythological statements in light of the self-understanding to which they point.

If Bultmann's insight that all knowledge is existentially based is

correct, it is also true that understanding cannot take place
without pre-understanding *(Vorverständnis)*. A common world
of existential experience must obtain between the author and the
reader (1964a:123f.). But the pre-understanding, because it is
existential, is always historically conditioned. So the linguistic
tradition which one brings to the text varies radically from one
situation to another. And any language in which the hearer
expresses his or her response remains only relatively adequate to
the existential reality to which it refers.

> Every theological explication of the salvation-event and of
> Christian existence arises within the conceptuality of the
> respective time. Since it is always also discourse about man and
> his world, it always works itself out in traditional
> anthropological and cosmological concepts. (1964a:263)

Thus within the New Testament itself we find widely varying
conceptual frameworks in which the meaning of the Christ-event
is articulated. Such variation is most evident in John's criticism
and reformulation of traditional eschatology (1961: 20; 1955:9f.).
But the discrepancy between John and the other New Testament
books is simply an exaggerated instance of a relativity which is
part and parcel of the process of transmitting tradition. The task
of the contemporary interpreter is not essentially different from
that of the interpreters who stand within the canon itself. Every
new situation demands a new interpretation. Interpretation
means the translation from one historical linguistic tradition to
another and, consequently, criticism of tradition: "Since such
concepts change in the course of time, neither Paul nor any
theology or Christology can be understood without criticism"
(1964a:263). There is therefore no final interpretation of the New
Testament—no abstractable essence which will be intelligible in
all times and places. For the reality to which it witnesses is
existential, not conceptual. In Kierkegaard's (5ff.) terms, it cannot
be grasped with the intellect in a final way and hence possessed. It
cannot be gained through recollection, for it is not a generally
available set of truths (Bultmann. 1964a:126). Thus

demythologizing cannot consist in merely subtracting the incredible elements in order to uncover an eternal essence. It is rather the interpretation of the mythological in thought-forms which are the substance of one's own contemporary situation (1961:3-10). And for Bultmann this means, more specifically, a translation of New Testament categories into the "existentials" of Martin Heidegger's *Being and Time*.

Bultmann's program of demythologizing claims both a general and a specific warrant from the New Testament itself. The general warrant is the historicity of all New Testament formulations. The New Testament is the first chapter in the ongoing history of. translating the Christian message into linguistic forms shaped by new historical situations. The specific warrant is the drive toward existential categories which is perceptible at various points in this process. It appears in all forms of the use of the language of address but less ambiguously in other ways—as, for instance, in Paul's "subjectivizing" of the crucifixion (Gal 2:10) and John's de-temporalizing of the prevailing salvation-history.

Critics have often charged Bultmann with imposing a modern point of view upon the New Testament. And it is true that he accepts unequivocally the advent of the modern world-view as the occasion of the self-conscious use of existential interpretation. An emphasis upon his warrants within the text should not be taken as a denial of his explicit modernity. He does not suppose that his recognition of the discrepancy between Paul's use of $\pi\nu\epsilon\hat{\nu}\mu\alpha$ and $\sigma\acute{\alpha}\rho\xi$ in their Gnostic senses and his affirmation of the unity of the human self belong only accidentally to the twentieth century, as if they might as easily have occurred in any other time. To the contrary, the necessity of an outlook in which these ways of thinking are split asunder is precisely what sets this age apart from all others. So the modern world-view does function as a hermeneutical tool: "It is, of course, true that demythologizing takes the modern world-view as a criterion. . . . To demythologize is to deny that the message of Scripture and of the Church is bound to an ancient world-view which is obsolete" (1958:35f.).

But it must be remembered that on Bultmann's view every occasion of interpretation entails the use of conceptualities distinctive to the situation of the interpreter. That modern criteria are used in understanding the text means only that interpretation is by nature historical. The demythologizing project may be conceived as a content-criticism in which the modern perception of the unity and responsibility of the human self is used as a criterion for freeing the New Testament from a frame of reference which is now seen to contradict its own basic intention. As such it stands squarely within the ongoing process of tradition.

It is important to note, finally, that Bultmann in no way denies the descriptive task of the interpreter. What he does deny is, first, that this task completes an understanding of the New Testament and, second, that it is totally separable from the attempt at "contemporization." Interpretation embraces an objectifying dimension and is theoretically possible from a standpoint outside any sort of faith-commitment to the vision of existence attested in the text. But a full understanding of the New Testament nevertheless demands that the interpreter approach it with openness and freedom (1951-, Vol. 2:241), for no one can really understand the message who does not experience the life-and-death issues to which it purports to speak.

In agreement with Bultmann, the proponents of the "new hermeneutic" hold that the descriptive task does not complete an understanding of the New Testament, that such an understanding can be achieved only by use of the categories of the interpreter's present, and that demythologizing is necessary for a proper reading of the New Testament in our time. But, drawing upon an understanding of language and reality developed in Heidegger's later writings, continued by Hans-George Gadamer, and paralleled in the works of Maurice Merleau-Ponty, they seek to understand the task of demythologizing in a still more radical fashion.

Bultmann's point of view involves both a positive and a negative valuation of language (see Funk: 23ff.), but proponents of the new hermeneutic wish to overcome the negative implications. In keeping with Bultmann's characterization of New Testament language as address, they argue that such discourse is to be distinguished sharply from discursive or informational language. The latter abstracts *from* being; the authentic form of the former is related *directly to* being. Language, in its primary sense, is not a system of symbols pointing to an already extant fund of meaning given in existence per se. Meaning is created concomitantly with the emergence of language. Language is thus the "house of being," which is to say its relationship to being is direct rather than indirect (*through* thought). Linguistic symbols point not to underlying concepts but to being. Their intention is not to order given concepts (to assert) but to draw the hearer into the realm of being which has evoked them.

Understanding therefore means less the appropriation of concepts through the intellect than existential encounter with the reality in which the speaker stands. In Robert Funk's words, "When language is pressed to its limits, it is discovered that speech is more than words or even content of words, that it is more than sentences composed of subject and predicate" (2). Or, as Merleau-Ponty puts it, meaning occurs not so much *in* words as *between* them (45). In a meaningful expression, the speaker stands in the presence of being and "shapes" words to express what he or she has "heard."

But there are times in the course of human history when "experience and thought . . . press the limits of *conventional* speech and spill over," when "language already understood" is found "inadequate to what is to be understood" (Funk: 2). In such a case, if meaning is to occur words must be shaken loose from their accumulated fund of conceptual meanings and placed into new contexts. Poetic speech is needed to jar the hearers loose from preoccupation with conventional conceptual meaning and draw them into the presence of being. When such a breakthough does occur, when a system of discursive language is disrupted by the presence of being and encounter takes place, we have a happening in the course of linguistic history which is termed a language-event or speech-event. Because language is so closely related to being, and because language is radically subject to the ebb and flow of history, it may be said that being itself has a history—the history of its emergence into and expulsion from language. Being is sometimes obscured by everyday language and sometimes breaks through encrusted speech. In either case it "makes history."

This understanding of language, it is claimed, obviates some of the difficulties inherent in the language tradition of Western thought. Most notably, it overcomes the "subject-object split" and the "tyranny of the subject"—i.e., the tendency of Western epistemology, since Descartes (and to some extent since Plato), so to emphasize the role of the experiencing subject as distinct from the object of perception that the very reality of the latter is actually called into question. While in the prevalent view the dominance of the subject as knower of an external object tends to result in the manipulation of experience by the subject, the "new" view of language, which actually draws its inspiration from pre-Socratic thought, stresses the inseparability of subject and object and hence the role of what is experienced in shaping the being of the one who experiences. While the prevalent view tends to reduce religious language to assertions which can be grasped as objects by an external subject, the newer view seeks to uncover the drive of such speech to penetrate the hearer's existence at its deepest level.

The proponents of the new hermeneutic find Bultmann guilty of falling prey to the traditional Western understanding of language. They charge that there is a hardened, non-existential element in his concept of kerygma, corresponding to his emphasis upon a constant in human nature. Funk (34), following Ebeling (42), notes the ambiguity of the term: at some points it means address, or preaching, but at other points it takes on the character of a doctrinal summation which appears when the mythological crust of the New Testament is penetrated.

If language is understood on the model proposed by the new hermeneutic, however, it becomes clear that the kerygmatic statements of the New Testament cannot stand alone as intelligible in themselves. The concepts appearing in them have no meaning apart from the historical reality to which they refer—no meaning apart from the primal language, the word-event, out of which they emerge. As Ebeling says, the linguistic elements in the kerygmatic statements of the New Testament are ambiguous. They lose their ambiguity only when they are interpreted in light of the concrete words and deeds of the historical Jesus who stands behind them (65).

If this understanding builds upon Bultmann's contention that all knowledge is existentially based, it also represents an important departure from his view. Bultmann does not deny that the historical Jesus may inform our understanding of the kerygma, but he sees the understanding of human reality presented in the kerygma as self-intelligible apart from any specific relationship to the historical Jesus. The historian's reconstruction apparently *may* inform us; nevertheless the kerygma *can* stand on its own apart from any such reconstruction. On the one hand this means that genuine understanding of the message of the text is existential: it occurs only when the interpreter shares the existential questions to which the message is addressed. But on the other hand these existential questions belong to human existence per se. This must be so if they are intelligible to all interpreters willing to question their own lives. A basic pre-understanding common to humanity in all times and places thus insures the intelligibility of the kerygma. But it is just this common pre-understanding that the language-model of the new hermeneutic challenges. If from this perspective a pre-understanding is necessary, it must be conceived as more radically historical than Bultmann would allow. Two crucial implications follow.

First, there can be little confidence in the use of systematized philosophical concepts in getting at the New Testament. The emphasis falls upon hearing the language of the text itself and ordering our own language accordingly. A system of concepts is, per se, subject to criticism, in Heideggerian fashion, as ready-to-hand and hence as impervious to the voice of being in history (Fuchs, 1960b:113f.). The system as such is an expression of the "tyranny of the subject."

Second, if a common pre-understanding is lacking, the

descriptive task has an even smaller place in this program than in Bultmann's. If the kerygmatic statements do not stand alone, we are driven to the historical Jesus. And if his words are unintelligible apart from the reality in which he stands, and that reality is itself a creature of history rather than a common denominator for all history, then his words are understood only by those who are drawn existentially into his sphere. So existential decision, or faith, becomes a hermeneutical tool (Fuchs, 1960b:78). Or, as Gadamer contends, to understand means to take what is understood for truth (278). If there is no universal pre-understanding, being is not universally available. And if being is not universally available, it can be encountered only when it emerges in a speech-event and draws the hearer into its presence.

The advance upon Bultmann is this: interpretation is a more radically existential endeavor in that it more directly involves the existential attitude of the interpreter. Demythologizing is still necessary, but it becomes a merely preliminary step to the more important process by which the language of the New Testament "interprets" or demythologizes" the interpreter's own mode of being (Funk: 49f.). Whereas for Bultmann the language of the text cannot exhaust the reality lying behind it, this language becomes in the new hermeneutic the very substance of the reality that is to be conveyed. It is Jesus' word which creates a universe of meaning where the hearer is invited to stand. To stand where he stands means to hear his word, and vice-versa. Far from obscuring reality, language—when it functions properly—actually opens it up. And if language must shift with the passage of time, this points not to its inadequacy but to its historicity, which is the ground of its ability to "speak being."

There is, in my estimation, some force to the contention that Bultmann merely reduces the conceptuality of one world-view to that of another. While it is hardly fair to say that Bultmann intends such a simplistic procedure, he has at least left himself open to the charge that the Heideggerian "existentials" simply constitute a new mythology that he grasps as tightly as first-century people grasped theirs. And he does tend to speak of the kerygma in quasi-doctrinal terms. Thus whoever seeks to defend

Bultmann must take responsibility for clarifying this point. And the resources of the Heidegger of *Being and Time* have hardly been proved adequate to this challenge.

It must be noted, however, that it is Bultmann's combination of a definable meaning of the demythologized text with the assumption of a constant pre-understanding given in human nature that explains the intelligibility of the Christian message in changing historical contexts. Thus whoever challenges Bultmann on this point is saddled with the problem of accounting for continuity in the ongoing tradition. And it is not entirely clear that the resources of the *later* Heidegger have been proved adequate on this score.

And if it is countered that the language-event creates its own world of meaning, the question is whether religious language is not condemned to a kind of experiential ghetto. If primal language is seen as so completely different from the discursive language of the everyday, this result would seem inevitable. To be sure, it is just this differentiation that is intended to overcome the "subject-object split" and to avoid the reduction of religious language to intellectualistic terms that can be "handled" by the interpreter. But when the rift between the types of language is made too great, we inevitably fall into the trap of linguistic solipsists. If religious language depends so heavily upon one's existential appropriation of it, then it is reduced to a discrete language game alongside other, equally discrete games based upon differing "bliks." It would seem that unless all modes of discourse have something in common at the most basic level, communication would simply be impossible. But an accounting of this common basis is what is notably lacking in the new hermeneutic. One problem with this perspective, then, is that it operates within a theological ghetto.

A second problem is that the new hermeneutic fails to take sufficient account of the negative possibilities of (even authentic) religious language. Dan Via has put the matter succinctly:

> If I do not understand a text because my own confused self-understanding does not permit me to grasp the pattern of

connections in the text, the text is still not understandable to
me. And if a second word is used to clarify my situation so that I
can understand the first word, then the first word is also being
illumined; and the fact remains that the first word by itself was
not able to clarify my situation. We may agree with Ebeling that
understanding finally came from a word and that we do not
escape the linguistic realm to attain understanding, but his
position, that language normally mediates understanding,
appears to be an abstraction from the fact that language is
always used and heard by people whose understanding of their
situation is to some extent clouded. (35)

Granted, then, that Bultmann's hermeneutic is problematic in that
it tends to reduce the thought-forms of one world-view to those of
another and thus to suppress some aspects of the text, the new
hermeneutic entails serious problems of its own. The question is
whether an approach can be developed which avoids both
Bultmann's tendency to reduce the text to those aspects of it which
fit a foreign conceptuality and the new hermeneutic's tendency to
render it intelligible only for an elite. It is at this point that I believe
the understanding of language that undergirds Whitehead's
metaphysics may be of some help.

There is an additional problem, too, common to both
Bultmann and the new hermeneutic, to which any new proposal
ought to speak. Clearly, the writers of the New Testament wish to
do more than reveal to their readers their own subjective feelings
about Jesus, God, or human nature. The entire New Testament is
shot through with truth-claims of both explicit and implicit
character. The writers go beyond mere assertion, to be sure; they
seek to address their readers and involve them in the truth they
have to convey. But the presupposition that clearly undergirds
their appeals is that what they have to say is in fact the truth. The
truth-claim, however, is a dimension of the text with which neither
Bultmann nor the new hermeneutic has adequately dealt /1/.

When, for example, Bultmann says that "The saving efficacy of
the cross is not derived from the fact that it is the cross of Christ: it
is the cross of Christ because it has this saving adequacy"
(1961:41), one may legitimately ask whether he has not reduced

the truth-claim of the New Testament to a matter of subjective prejudice. As for the new hermeneutic, the problem is even more evident: it stresses the poetic and non-discursive nature of religious speech to such an extent that one wonders whether any place at all is left for the claim to truth. It is my hope to show that a process hermeneutic, based upon Whitehead's understanding of language, can render this claim intelligible without obscuring the character of the text as address.

Chapter 2

Prospectus for a Process Hermeneutic

To understand Whitehead's view of language, one must first take account of his general epistemology. In his estimation, the fundamental error of Western epistemology lies in its identification of sense-data as the basis of all perception (1929: 198-237). Whitehead himself is convinced that more basic than sense-perception, which he terms "perception in the mode of presentational immediacy," is a primal awareness of our relationship to the causal nexus in which we exist. This he names "perception in the mode of causal efficacy."

As evidence of this latter mode, Whitehead points to two aspects of human awareness. First, there is our memory of our own immediately past state of consciousness. Although this might indeed be memory of sense-experience, the memory itself is not derived from the senses:

> Let us elaborate the consideration of the angry man. His anger is the subjective form of his feeling for some datum D. A quarter of a second later he is, consciously, or unconsciously, embodying his past as a datum in the present, and maintaining in the present the anger which is a datum from the past. In so far as that feeling has fallen within the illumination of consciousness, he enjoys a non-sensuous perception of past emotion. (1933:185f.)

The second indication of non-sensuous perception is a vague awareness of our own bodies as elements in a causal nexus moving from past to present to future:

> In this division of experience there are the sense of derivation from without, the sense of immediate enjoyment within, and the sense of transmission beyond. This complex sense of enjoyment involves the past, the present, the future. It is the realization of our essential connection with the world without,

and also of our individual existence now. It carries with it the
placing of our immediate experience as a fact in history,
derivative, actual, and effective. (1935:235f.)

As lower forms of life, although devoid of sense organs, are able to
react to their environments, just so do we possess a primal
awareness of ourselves as a part of an environment (1929: 268)
/2/.

The obvious rejoinder on this point is that we are indeed aware
of our environment—precisely through our senses. But
Whitehead argues that the sense organ does not merely deliver
perceptions of the external world. Scarcely noticed, because of the
overwhelming clarity and precision of sense-perceptions, is a
concomitant awareness of the organ of perception itself
(1929:268). We do not merely feel things; we feel ourselves feeling
them. We are thus aware of our bodies themselves in a prior sense.
And that the diverse organs of the body are able to order sense
experience by channeling it into the brain can mean only that we
have a primal sense of bodily unity on the basis of which
coordination takes place. "There is thus every reason," he aruges,

> to believe that our sense of unity with the body has the same
> origin as our sense of unity with our immediate past of personal
> experience. It is another case of non-sensuous perception, only
> now devoid of the strict personal order. (1933:243f.)

Although there is a kind of direct recognition that takes place in
each mode of perception individually considered, what we mean
by "perception" actually involves a symbolic reference—i.e., a
synthesis of the two modes. Presentational immediacy *refers to*
causal efficacy; the latter places the former in a context of
meaning (1929:255-79; 1927b: *passim*). And clearly, on this
model, symbolic reference cannot take place without valuation,
for it consists precisely in the ordering of bare sense-data in terms
of a larger nexus within which they achieve a particular relevance:

> It must be distinctly understood that no prehension, even of
> bare sensa, can be divested of its affective tone, that is to say of

its character of "concern" in the Quaker sense. Concernedness
is of the essence of perception. (1933:232)

Already on the basis of this general analysis of perception, it can
be seen that the dichotomy between subject and object has been
relativized, but not obliterated. To say that we are aware of
ourselves as related to a larger causal nexus is to imply, first of all,
that our perceptions are based upon data external to ourselves.
What we are aware of, in part, is a causal past distinct from our
immediate subjectivity. We remember the immediate past as past;
we feel objects as something other than our hands. Yet it is also
clear that no experience can take place apart from the
appropriation of causal forces in terms of our own subjective
immediacy which defines their meanings. We perceive the datum,
always and only, in relation to a particular significance it has for
us. Whitehead's epistemology, then, involves a concept of
participatory knowledge, which represents one aspect of his
broader metaphysical doctrine of internal relations (1929:471).

The point is that Whitehead has restored the causal world
against Hume's protests and forced the phenomenal world back
upon Descartes. From his perspective, the very act of perception
implies a world of real causal relations which occur through
participation and valuation. The subject does not grasp the object
with its rational capacities alone; nor does the object become a
pawn in the hands of an angry or arbitrary subject. Without
compressing one pole of the subject-object schema into the other,
Whitehead has in his own way overcome the "subject-object split"
and the "tyranny of the subject" that so concern the
Heideggerians.

If perception is understood on Whitehead's model, the
language which emerges from it will of necessity be seen as
analogical. This means that words can never be taken in a
univocal sense, as if they referred to absolutely definite objects.
Such definiteness would be impossible, since an analysis of
perception itself discloses not a world of discrete objects but a
fluid environment made up of myriads of causal nexūs.
(Whitehead uses nexūs as the plural of nexus.) Effects are

internally related to their causes; events, entities, are what they are by virtue of the broader contexts within which they stand. Words, then, are characterized by a necessary inexactness, and Whitehead can speak of language as "incomplete and fragmentary" (1933:291-93; see also 287).

The application of name to an object always entails the process of lifting some aspects of a reality out of the complex and dynamic set of relationships within which it occurs. Conversely, other aspects of the reality are ignored: "The essence of language is that it utilizes those elements in experience most easily abstracted for conscious entertainment, and most easily reproduced in experience" (1938:48; see also 54f.). Consequently, linguistic forms are necessarily abstract, because, in Lyman Lundeen's words, "they do not indicate their connection with a concrete perspective, purpose, or process," but are "treated as though they were independent of their contextual relationships" (29).

Since language is necessarily "incomplete and fragmentary," no linguistic formulation ever expresses fully that which lies behind it—a proposition (or set of propositions), which is defined as the possibility of some pure potentiality (eternal object, the predicate of the proposition) to be realized in some actuality (actual entity, the logical subject of the proposition) (1929:393f.). Moreover, the function of a proposition is primarily that of a "lure toward feeling." To be sure, the "feelings" toward which the prehending subject of the proposition (the entity that "entertains" the proposition by "feeling" it in a particular way) is drawn are not simply affective in the popular sense of that term. They are precisely those encounters with actualities and potentialities that form the basis of all experience. But the point is, nevertheless, that Whitehead explicitly contrasts the role of the "lure toward feeling" with that of a conveyer of logical precision or truth:

It is evident that the primary function of theories is as a lure for feeling, thereby providing immediacy of enjoyment and purpose. Unfortunately theories, under their name of "propositions," have been handed over to logicians, who have countenanced the doctrine that their one function is to be judged as to their truth or falsehood. (1929:281)

Propositions do of course call for truth-judgments (1929:392), and these too are feelings. But the truth-judgment is but one among many types of feelings elicited by propositions (1929:396). "Immediacy of enjoyment and purpose" are broader categories; the basal encounter with the subject and predicate of the proposition is the real focus of interest. According to Whitehead, then, "it is more important that a proposition be interesting than that it be true. The importance of truth is, that it adds to interest" (1929:396). Thus the actual function of language cannot be reduced to the production of univocal significations that can be pronounced true or false.

If language on Whitehead's model is imprecise and analogical, it is also value-laden. The process of abstraction necessary for the formation of a word is anything but a cold and unfeeling activity. It takes place only because a felt value is already at work in the very act of discriminating an object for naming. So the meaning of a word does not lie in the word itself in a simplistic sense; meaning depends upon a host of what Lundeen terms "non-linguistic factors" which provide words with specific references and intentions—which is to say, with particular values. Abstracting cannot take place without an end in view. And this means, finally, that for Whitehead all language involves some level of commitment (Lundeen: 48, 71, 77, 103).

Whitehead is not oblivious to the way in which language can suffer a relative loss of immediacy so that the value-dimension is obscured. But for him the culprit is not abstraction, since this is a prerequisite for all language. Nor can language ever lose its value-dimension totally, since the process of valuation is built into that of abstraction. What can happen, however, is that we ignore the value-oriented abstraction that has taken place and treat words as if they signified in a univocal sense (Lundeen: 67). When this happens, we do indeed treat objects as self-contained, self-defined, and valueless entities:

> For example, single words, each with its dictionary meaning, and single sentences, each bounded by full stops, suggest the possibility of complete abstraction from any environment.

Thus the problem of philosophy is apt to be conceived as the understanding of the interconnectedness of things, each understandable, apart from reference to anything else. (1938:90)

Is this not a description of the "tyranny of the subject?" In Whitehead's terms, though, such a misunderstanding comes under the rubric of the "fallacy of misplaced concreteness" (Lundeen: 62f.). For it arises from our refusal to acknowledge the degree of abstraction involved in the formation of the terms we are using. The cure for this malady is the recognition of propositions for what they fundamentally are—lures for feeling, which point beyond themselves to prior experiences of a complex and dynamic nature.

Now this understanding of language in general has two important consequences with respect to religious language. In the first instance, it means that religious language can be valued positively. Just because words never refer to absolutely definite and discrete objects, but point analogically to elements abstracted from a continuous flow of experience, every assertion ultimately presupposes and points toward a larger whole, an encompassing process that embraces all experience: "The point is that every proposition refers to a universe exhibiting some general systematic metaphysical characteristics" (1929:16). Since metaphysics and religious language deal, in different ways, explicitly with this larger whole, they perform essential functions (1926:143ff.). If they are subjective and value-laden, the same is also true in some measure of all thinking and speaking—even that which claims the highest degree of objectivity. To this extent they simply share the generic characteristics of all language. But their unique value lies in making explicit what is merely implicit in all other modes of speech: an understanding of and a commitment to a particular vision of the ultimate nature of things.

In the second instance, Whitehead's general view of language means that religious language (like all other modes of discourse) may nevertheless be misleading. The problem arises when the arbiters of any language misunderstand its nature—specifically, when they take it to be literal rather than analogical. When a religion takes its faith-statements as dogmas, as denoting the content of faith in a direct, precise, literal fashion, then it distorts the relationship between language and faith (1927a:145). Properly understood, religious statements (like all other statements) are primarily lures for feeling. But, in order to signify, religious language tends to present its terms as if they were precise: hence an overwhelming temptation to treat religious statements as literal. For this reason, religious language shares with other modes of speech the need for metaphysical clarification (1927a:78). Even metaphysical language itself, however, is not exempt from the "dogmatic fallacy," but must be bracketed by an acknowledgment of the ultimate inadequacy of its categories: "The position of metaphysics in the development of culture cannot be understood without remembering that no verbal statement is the adequate expression of a proposition" (1929:20). Metaphysics, too, is subject to the ongoing process of criticism and clarification.

It should be apparent that Whitehead's understanding of language is in some respects similar to that which the proponents of the new hermeneutic have derived from Heidegger and Merleau-Ponty /3/. From both perspectives, at least some forms of language are seen as primarily evocative in nature. But important differences remain. From the perspective of the new hermeneutic, it would seem that the discursive language of the everyday must be sharply distinguished from the primal language with which the authentically religious speak. For Whitehead, however, this distinction is relativized, since all language shares, in some measure, this evocative character.

It would appear, then, that Whitehead's perspective promises to overcome the problem indicated by my first criticism of the new hermeneutic. While Whitehead appreciates the power of language to draw the hearer into a circle of understanding and say something new, he does not assume that language must do all the work. The non-linguistic factors which give words their specific content not only define an immediate experiential context, but also point beyond themselves to a larger whole of which the immediate context is but a transient part. The ultimate reason a word can bring about understanding is that it is spoken within the framework of an intelligible universe, and for Whitehead it is finally this that guarantees the possibility of communication.

The implication is that every human being has, by virtue of living in and experiencing the world, some feeling for the reference of religious symbols. For all the modes of discourse in which we are involved engage us in valuation and so point ultimately to a metaphysical ground of value. This feeling, of course, is of a formal nature and does not insure that any given person will appropriate the content of the symbols by an act of explicit faith. But it does mean that all persons, by virtue of their humanity, have the basic equipment, in however rudimentary a form, with which to make that appropriation.

In all fairness, it should be noted that both Merleau-Ponty and Heidegger do take account of elements in the process of understanding that seem to correspond to Whitehead's "nonlinguistic factors" /4/. Merleau-Ponty, for example, can speak of a primordial "silence" which forms the background for the rise of speech and a field of reference which gives it meaning:

> If we want to do justice to expressive speech, we must evoke some of the other expressions which might have taken its place and were rejected, and we must feel the way in which they might have touched and shaken the chain of language in another manner and the extent to which this particular expression was the only possible one if that signification was to come into the world. In short, we must consider the speech before it is spoken, the background of silence which does not cease to surround it and without which it would say nothing. (46)

Thus if language does not presuppose a rigid set of correspondents which lie beneath each expression but rather "unveils its secrets itself" (43), this cannot be taken to mean that language creates meaning *ex nihilo*. The statement that "meaning appears only at the intersection of and as it were in the interval between words" (42), even though intended to deny an exact reference for every word, actually implies a non-exact "background" out of which speech arises and to which it refers.

Heidegger treads upon similar ground in *Being and Time* when he argues that the "traditional" concept of truth as belonging to an assertion actually presupposes a primordial truth which inheres in entities themselves (256-73, especially 266). This primordial truth functions as the locus of assertion, and thus the demonstration of the truth of an assertion means the demonstration of its ability to "uncover" the primordial truth to which it refers. "What gets demonstrated is the Being-uncovering of the assertion" (261). And the primordial truth that is "uncovered" is given the explicit role of forming the background against which assertion takes shape:

> Assertion is not the primary "locus" of truth. *On the contrary,* whether as a mode in which uncoveredness is appropriated or as a way of Being-in-the-world, assertion is grounded in Dasein's uncovering, or rather in *disclosedness.* The most primordial "truth" is the "locus" of assertion; it is the ontological condition for the possibility that assertions can be either true or false—that they may uncover or cover things up. (269)

This would seem to indicate that words necessarily refer to a prior reality which gives them shape and import, since "the roots of the truth of assertion reach back to the disclosedness of the understanding" (266).

The crucial difference, though, is that Whitehead takes the grounding of human language in something beyond itself as an invitation to metaphysical thought, whereas Merleau-Ponty and Heidegger (particularly in his later thought) draw exactly the opposite conclusion. The reason, of course, is that they recognize that no discursive formulation can capture the essence of primordial reality. Thus what is appropriate in the presence of being is not conceptual clarification but "essential thinking," which "answers to the demands of Being" (Heidegger, 1949:389-92). And Whitehead, too, acknowledges the limitation of discursive speech precisely in his insistence that language refers to a dynamic reality it can never envelop. But he also sees that the task of discursive clarification cannot be forfeited altogether without denying the unity of the human person and the intelligibility of reality. While Heidegger and Merleau-Ponty bring us to the brink of a metaphysics and leave us dangling, Whitehead sees that the metaphysical question arises within the language problem itself. And if Heidegger and Merleau-Ponty are perceptive in their recognition of a "primordial silence," they miss its implications for an appreciation of everyday speech: if such a factor is indeed at work in the formation of speech, then one wonders how primal language and everyday speech can be severed so neatly. Whitehead would seem to follow his own insights more consistently.

As to my second criticism of the new hermeneutic, it should be clear that Whitehead's perspective can provide a more adequate account of the negative possibilities inherent in religious language. For Whitehead, the problem with any language system lies in its tendency to present itself as if it signified univocally. What is all-important in this connection is that Whitehead is able to take account of the way in which mythological language can evoke faith and deceive the hearer simultaneously. To recognize the deceptive tendency in religious language is not, as the Heideggerians seem to think, to reduce it to an objectified and bloodless pawn in human hands. For this tendency grows out of that tension between evocation and signification common to all speech, a tension which is the root not only of deception but of the existential power of speech as well.

Rather than reducing religous speech to the discursive language of the everyday, then, Whitehead has exposed the dialectic of the everyday and the radically new, the univocal and the analogical, the precise and the provocative, that constitutes both the beauty and the problematic of all modes of discourse. No form of speech is inherently authentic or inauthentic. With respect to religious language, the matter hinges upon the way in which one hears what is spoken, the way in which one treats and understands the confession to which he or she relates. It would seem, indeed, that Whitehead's perspective could provide a ready framework for a comprehensive explication of the duality Bultmann discovered in the mythological language of the New Testament.

What I should like to propose in terms of a process hermeneutic is not the direct translation of New Testament categories into those of process metaphysics, but simply that Whitehead's view of language be used to inform our appreciation of the nature of the text. Clearly, a Whiteheadian understanding of religious language will relate positively to Bultmann's demythologizing project, because Whitehead and Bultmann have this much in common in their theories of language: for both, religious discourse refers, at least in part, to the life-experiences in which we, as hearers, are already involved by virtue of our humanity-in-the-world. For Bultmann, this is expressed in the concept of "pre-understanding." In Whiteheadian terms, the same point is implied by the contention that religious language shares a common root and common nature with other modes of discourse. And it is this perspective that will free a process hermeneutic from the problems entailed in the new hermeneutic's claim that the text interprets the reader. For the process interpreter will recognize that a) interpretation is always relatively distinct from human response to the word of the text but also that b) all understanding is rooted in a measure of personal involvement, so that c) faith and/or concern may indeed aid interpretation, while interpretation may in turn enhance the evocation of human response.

A process hermeneutic will, however, entail an advance upon Bultmann in that it will avoid the impression that demythologizing consists in the simple reduction of the terms of one language game to those of another. To this limited extent it will parallel the new hermeneutic and could provide a bridge between Bultmann's rather negative appreciation of mythology and the more positive evaluations of Eliade and Ricoeur /5/. A Whiteheadian model should make clear that every re-statement of a traditional religious message is also by nature imprecise and analogical in the sense that all language can be so described. Thus there should be no question of understanding the kerygma as hardened doctrine or of replacing the primal images of the text with a discursive statement pleasing to the modern ear. But just because it is seen that religious language parallels ordinary language at this point, interpretation need not tend toward the experiential exclusiveness of the new hermeneutic.

What a process hermeneutic implies, concretely, is a bifocal approach to the text. Interpretation on this model will involve two relatively distinct but complementary movements. Because the language of the text is imprecise and analogical, the interpreter must work through the discursive implications of the text back to the complex of feelings toward which it lures the reader. But if it is also true that religious language presupposes metaphysical commitments, then the basal lure of the text will reveal a fundamental disposition toward reality itself. So the interpreter must also trace the broadest presuppositions of the address embodied in the text. Thus a process methodology should also avoid the tendency of both Bultmann and the new hermeneutic to suppress the truth-claim of the text under the weight of existential interpretation. But it will point the reader beyond surface assertions to the *ultimate* claim to truth upon which the lure finally rests. Just because process interpretation recognizes the common root of all language, it is open to the "metaphysical" dimension of the text, which transcends the immediate confessional appeal, whenever it does in fact appear.

This does not mean that process interpreters must begin with rigid metaphysical commitments, but only that they must be sensitive to the broadest implications inherent in the lures that the text embodies. Precisely because all language is "incomplete and fragmentary," the implicit understanding of reality in general, like the basal image given in the text, always appears as a question (or theory), a possibility for understanding existence. Image and presupposition, then, are two aspects of an integral whole in which a value-judgment, as well as a truth-judgment, is called for. Were this not the case, religious discourse could simply be replaced by a univocally-understood metaphysics. But it is just because such a univocal metaphysics is impossible that religious speech arises.

NOTES

/1/   It may legitimately be pointed out that the perspective of the new hermeneutic is grounded upon an understanding of "truth" quite at variance with the Western correspondence theory (see, e.g., Heidegger, 1962:256-73). While I believe Whitehead's own notion of truth has some affinities with Heidegger's, it should be noted that unless the element of correspondence is given some place, human communication becomes impossible. For if a truth-claim is in no sense verifiable, outside some kind of mystical experience, then all claims become esoteric. What, after all, is the search for correspondence, if not an attempt "to place. . . one's experience in the context of the universe which embraces one's *total* experience and that of other experiencing creatures" (Pregeant, 1970:24)? Granted that the truth of an assertion is grounded in something outside itself, the point is that the truth or falsehood of the assertion itself can be determined only by asking whether it corresponds to the reality about which it asserts something. And presupposed in the asking of this question is the partial accessibility of that reality to universal human experience and to conceptual categories.

/2/   "It does not seem to be the sense of causal awareness that the lower things lack, so much as a variety of sense-presentation, and the vivid distinctness of presentational immediacy. But animals, and even vegetables, in low forms of organism exhibit modes of behaviour directed towards self-preservation. There is every indication of a vague feeling of causal relationship with the external world, of some intensity, vaguely defined as to quality, and with some vague definition as to locality. A jellyfish advances and withdraws, and in so doing exhibits some perception of causal relationship with the world beyond itself; a plant grows downwards to the damp earth, and upwards toward the light. There is thus some direct reason for attributing dim, slow feelings of causal nexus, although we have no reason for any ascription of the definite percepts in the mode of presentational immediacy" (1929:268).

/3/   To this extent it is also similar to that of Ian Ramsey.

/4/   I am indebted to Schubert Ogden for this insight, although I do not of course wish to hold him responsible for my particular development of it.

/5/   Norman Perrin has suggested that the varying views regarding mythology held by Bultmann, Eliade, and Ricoeur, although quite divergent, may nevertheless be viewed as complementary rather than contradictory (21-26).

Part II

Outline for an Experimental Venture: Christology and Soteriology in Matthew's Gospel

Chapter 3

My purpose is to test the methodology I have proposed by applying it to an exegetical issue. The problematic aspect of such an attempt at validation is of course that hermeneutical stance in part determines exegetical results. There is thus, even in principle, no way to make an objective incision in the hermeneutical circle, no way to achieve a neutral point of departure in order to make the test intended.

But all methodology, in the final analysis, is stuck with the same problem. And despite the necessary circularity of procedure, two criteria of evaluation do suggest themselves. For lack of a standard nomenclature, I shall term them "depth" and "appropriateness." By the first I mean the ability of any given method to expose various "layers" of signification—i.e., to demonstrate the presence in the text of meanings not perceptible by the angles of vision provided by other means. This is a somewhat slippery notion, to be sure, and the testing of "depth" must be buttressed by sound evidence of a scientific nature. That is to say, the results of a methodology designed to get at layers of signification that lie beneath the surface meaning must be shown to stand in basic continuity with that surface meaning as demonstrable by the accepted exegetical tools. In the end, of course, the criteria must be correlative. For the surface meaning may appear in a different light once a new approach is taken in order to expose the deeper levels.

By speaking of "appropriateness" I mean to indicate that the text itself should provide some evidence that the model through which it is approached reflects an actual aspect of the text's construction. In the present case, for example, I should think it incumbent upon me to demonstrate that the New Testament exhibits the dual characteristics Whitehead finds in religious language: fragmentariness and metaphysical thrust. Such characteristics can admittedly be found only if they are sought. But the decision not to seek them is equally as subjective as the decision to do so. For every hermeneutical method, the process of interpretation involves alternation between subjective and objective perspectives.

The particular problem I have chosen to investigate is one that has direct bearing upon the hermeneutical problem. For that reason it is both doubly difficult and doubly important as a test of the methodology under consideration. The question, simply put, is whether the christology of the New Testament may legitimately be read in a fully existential way—i.e., whether its deepest intention is served or distorted by understanding it as a cipher for a particular vision of the human possibility before God, rather than as an assertion regarding an exclusive and once-for-all act of God in behalf of human salvation /1/.

According to Herbert Braun, the three major theological components of the New Testament—the teachings of Jesus, the letters of Paul, and the gospel of John—contain a constant anthropology, or conception of the character of authentic human existence. This anthropology may be summed up in the assertion that human life is defined by the dual aspects of the proclamation under which it stands: radical grace and radical demand. On the other hand, christology does not appear to be a constant among these three, since Jesus does not present a christology and those of Paul and John are differently conceived. Moreover, the differences in conceptuality also show that the shared anthropology has not been passed on historically. While christology varies, the anthropology—which is not communicated *as such*—remains constant.

Braun draws an important conclusion from these observations: the constant factor in the New Testament is not christology, but anthropology. The self-understanding contained in the New

Testament actually has an independent significance. For not only does it appear outside the Christian proclamation (in the ministry of Jesus himself), but as the constant factor which appears apart from historical transmission it becomes the standard by which christology is judged, rather than vice-versa.

Ernst Käsemann, however, disputes Braun's conclusion with the contention that "Hardly anywhere in the New Testament, except in Paul and to a smaller degree in the gospel of John, is there any explicit anthropology at all" (44). Thus with the vast majority of New Testament scholars he holds that the unifying factor in the New Testament is indeed the witness to the Christ-event as a unique act of God in behalf of human salvation.

It can hardly be denied that Käsemann is correct in the sense that the formal fact of a christological witness is indeed a constant in the New Testament. But it is quite revealing that he qualifies his denial of anthropology with partial concessions in the instances of Paul and John and further with the term "explicit." The real question is not whether the various New Testament authors develop explicit and systematic statements on human nature but whether the discrepancies among their christological formulations justify the reduction of their christologies to the common anthropology Braun has convincingly exposed. The anthropology Käsemann misses is to be found just beneath the surface of the christology he acknowledges; the question is whether one chooses to subject the latter to a critique informed by existential categories. So the issue between Braun and Käsemann is in the end hermeneutical rather than exegetical.

The same question is posed in a different way by Schubert Ogden's attempt to carry Bultmann's demythologizing project through to its logical conclusion. On the one hand, Bultmann contends that the New Testament itself demands a fully non-mythological, existential, or anthropological interpretation and that its message, from such a perspective, appears as a witness to a particular human self-understanding, rather than to an instance of supernatural intervention in the world. On the other hand, however, he maintains that the New Testament's assertion of the emergence of a factually new human possibility, in and through the Christ-event, is a necessary component of its witness. What Ogden argues is that the witness to a literally *new* human possibility necessarily entails the notion of an exclusive act of God and is therefore non-existential and hence, on Bultmann's own terms, mythological.

Now Bultmann continually speaks of the Christ-event proclaimed in the New Testament in such a way as to imply its independent significance:

> In its redemptive aspect the cross of Christ is no mere mythical event, but a historic *(geschichtlich)* fact originating in the historical *(historisch)* event which is the crucifixion of Jesus. The abiding significance of the cross is that it is the judgment of the world, the judgment and deliverance of man. . . . In the last resort mythological language is only a medium for conveying the significance of the historical *(historisch)* event. The historical *(historisch)* event of the cross has, in the significance peculiar to it, created a new historic *(geschicht-lich)* situation. (1961:37)

The New Testament, he says, "claims that faith only became possible at a definite point in history in consequence of an *event*—viz., the event of Christ" (1961:22). But Bultmann denies that this claim entails a mythological concept: "To believe in the cross of Christ does not mean to concern ourselves with a mythical process wrought outside of us and our world, but rather to make the cross of Christ our own, to undergo crucifixion with him" (1961:36). The meaning of the event is not objectively verifiable, but is apparent only to the eyes of faith:

> It is precisely its immunity from proof which secures the Christian proclamation against the charge of being mythological. The transcendence of God is not as in myth reduced to immanence. Instead, we have the paradox of a transcendent God present and active in history: "The Word became flesh." (1961:44)

The question, however, is whether the assertion that faith became possible only at one point in history does not contradict the claim that faith is an existential possibility. Regardless of whether the proclamation is or is not "immune from proof," the claim that it is the *only* point in history at which faith is rendered possible would seem to set this event aside as an "act of God" in a very special sense. At this point Bultmann refers to the notion of paradox, claiming that, according to the New Testament, while authentic existence is *theoretically* available to humanity per se, it is *factually* available only in and through a particular event in history (1961:29). But Ogden argues that Bultmann's paradox is nothing more than a logical inconsistency:

> If Christian existence is a possibility belonging to man qua man, and so is something for which he is always responsible—and this is clearly what Bultmann wants to affirm when he says it is a "possibility in principle"—then, in this case at least, the distinction between "possibility in principle" and "possibility in fact" is vacuous. On the other hand, if this distinction is not vacuous but has a positive meaning, then the possibility in question is not an original possibility of man as such that he is always obligated to realize. This can be easily demonstrated.
>
> If, as seems self-evident, the only possibilities one may be held accountable for realizing (or not realizing) are genuine alternatives between which he can actually choose, then to the extent that Christian existence is a possibility for whose realization man is responsible, it is a genuine option open to his decision. Recognizing that Bultmann explicitly holds that to be "in" faith or "outside" it are possibilities for which man has full responsibility, we cannot avoid the conclusion that the distinction between "in principle" and "in fact" is completely empty when applied to Christian existence. Unless such existence is a "possibility in fact" as well as a "possibility in principle," it cannot be a possibility that man is accountable for realizing—although this, *ex hypothesi,* is exactly what it is. (1961:118)

Now Ogden's argument at this point is systematic rather than exegetical. But in that he clearly intends his constructive theological position as an interpretation of the New Testament itself, his argument against the validity of Bultmann's distinction between "possibility in principle" and "possibility in fact" reveals an aspect of his hermeneutical stance. He rejects the exclusivity of the Christ-event, as presented in the New Testament, because he finds it logically incompatible with other aspects of the New Testament's witness—i.e., the assumption of human responsbility and an emphasis upon God's universal love. He is thus quite insistent that his position expresses the deepest intention of the New Testament itself:

> To affirm, as is so often done, particularly by Protestant theologians, that the faith of the New Testament is "christocentric" is significantly to alter the New Testament's express emphasis. From its standpoint, the assertion that faith is "christocentric" is at best an elliptical assertion and, like other such assertions, constantly susceptible to misunderstanding and distortion. Unless it is made clear that "we are Christ's," but that "Christ is God's" (I Cor 3:23; cf.11:3), that is, unless the *theocentric* basis and sanction of "christocentrism" is explicitly acknowledged, emphasis upon Jesus Christ can be a share and a delusion and a mere travesty of authentic apostolic faith. (1961:143) /2/

According to Ogden, then, Bultmann in effect identifies the intention of the New Testament, quite rightly, as the re-presentation of the original possibility of authentic human existence (Ogden, 1961:112). But what Bultmann does not see is that insofar as the New Testament also claims that the Christ-event *creates* this possibility it is using mythological language which actually contradicts its own presuppositions regarding human freedom and responsibility. Thus the New Testament's presentation of the Christ-event must itself be demythologized, for "the only final condition" of authentic existence the New Testament consistently presents is one "that can be formulated in complete abstraction from the event Jesus of Nazareth and all that it specifically imports" (1961:143).

Herbert Braun, apparently, does not interpret his own conclusions in such a way as to give explicit support to Ogden's position. As Boers writes,

> According to Braun . . . authentic existence was realized *only* there [in the ministry of Jesus] in addition to its being a

response to the proclamation of Christ. In a considerable part of his work he attempted to determine what the distinctive character of the New Testament understanding of man was, including the understanding of man in the ministry of Jesus, in contrast with that of its environment, and concluded that it was precisely the characteristics of the human self-understanding of Jesus, Paul, and John which remained constant, which also distinguished them from their environment. . . .(39)

So one effect of Braun's contentions is actually to support Bultmann's paradoxical position by demonstrating that the Christian understanding of existence was unique in its original environment. And Bultmann readily approves Braun's line of argument (1964b:35f.).

The question toward which this study is directed, however, is not the historical question of whether authentic existence was or was not realized in any particular circumstance, but rather the exegetical question of what the fundamental witness of the New Testament is /3/. And in claiming that the anthropology of the New Testament is more basic than its christology, Braun lends implicit support to Ogden's "revision" of Bultmann's project.

Ogden has, it seems to me, exposed a real problem in Bultmann's theological stance. It is in fact difficult to make logical sense of the distinction between "possibility in principle" (or theoretical possibility) and "possibility in fact" (or factual possibility). And Thomas Oden's reference to Reinhold Niebuhr's distinction between the "necessity" and the "inevitability" of sin simply transfers the same difficulty to another set of terms /4/. But the fact remains, as Boers comments, that Bultmann's paradox

> is apparently a valid expression of what is the *typical* claim of the New Testament.
> If there is a difficulty here, it is with the New Testament, and not one for which Bultmann can be held responsible. And if we find it necessary to question this claim, our argument has to be with the New Testament. (5)

The New Testament, in other words, maintains just what Bultmann says it does—that humanity, apart from a special revelation, has the possibility of authentic existence only theoretically; but that in Jesus Christ the theoretical possibility has become factual.

But Ogden's contention, it must be remembered, is that he is carrying Bultmann's demythologizing project through to its logical conclusion. His point is that while a surface reading of the New Testament does in fact disclose a christocentric emphasis, Bultmann's own method of existential interpretation gives the interpreter the right to read that emphasis in terms of its existential import. Bultmann, of course, claims that he is doing just that, since he is not seeking to *prove* the revelatory nature of the Christ-event. But he is satisfied with an existential rendering which includes a paradoxical element, while Ogden is not. And each can claim the witness of the New Testament on his side— Bultmann because the paradox is embedded in the text itself and Ogden because one end of the paradox renders its opposite ineffective. The question, then, is what interpreters must do when they encounter a paradox in the text. Must they take due note of it and proclaim the interpretive process complete? Or is it legitimate to play one element off against another—i.e., to perform a thoroughgoing content-criticism on the very structure of the New Testament witness? How, in other words, does one decide whether a paradox is admissable in existential interpretation?

If the question seems unanswerable, this is in my estimation a sign of the inadequacy of Bultmann's language-model. The basic insight underlying the demythologizing project is sound: the New Testament is undoubtedly intended as an existential address, yet it employs a mode of speech that obscures the existential thrust. But the distinctions between address and information and between existential and mythological leave unsolved the question as to the admissability of paradox. While I agree with Ogden that once having begun the project of demythologizing—which is, after all, based upon the perception of inconsistency—Bultmann has no right to cut it off arbitrarily, one can nevertheless argue with some force that some human experiences transcend the categories of the mind and can be grasped only through the juxtaposition of apparently contradictory statements. Thus if it can be shown that the fundamental experience to which the New Testament attests is of such nature, interpretation must acquiesce and leave the readers to do with the paradox what they will. But the problem is that it is precisely the fundamental witness of the text that is in question. And Bultmann's language-model does not seem sufficiently comprehensive to get us beyond the impasse. Ogden can speak of inconsistency and Bultmann can speak of paradox; and each can apparently interpret the model in such a way as to support his own position. The existential method of interpretation is apparently fraught with ambiguity. And this ambiguity, together with the questions already raised regarding Bultmann's method, would seem to warrant the attempt to approach the text from another perspective.

The work of Hendrikus Boers on the question raised by Ogden and Braun constitutes, I believe, an important step toward a more comprehensive method and a more satisfactory solution. Boers has made an explicit attempt to interpret the New Testament witness to salvation in and through Jesus Christ in light of a universal possibility of authentic existence, stating bluntly that "the Christian claim that a true realization of man in the world is possible only in Christ cannot be maintained" (1). His method consists in looking beyond the intentions of the New Testament writers to the total thought-complexes with which they are engaged:

> A fundamental consideration of the study is that a text is not so much a product of thought, but a reproduction of a thought process, in so far as it is not itself a written thinking process. And the thinker is not the subject, but the predicate of a thinking process. . . .Thus, ultimately, we must come to ask, not only what the author of a text intended, but what happened to him in the writing of the text. (IX)

This sensitivity to what happens to an author allows Boers to examine the presuppositions which actually shape the development of the text but may not be explicitly stated. He thus finds that although the New Testament as a whole endorses a christological exclusivism, there are at least two points in New

Testament christology at which this exclusivism breaks down—the judgment scene in Matt 25:31-46 and Paul's treatment of the faith of Abraham in Rom 4. In each case the author's train of thought leads him to transcend the christological witness he intends to present.

The basic insight at work here is one I can appreciate, but David Dungan has raised an important objection:

> Basically, the conclusions drawn from the . . . examples seem quite far-fetched. One has the impression of a studious effort to comb *Das Kapital* for a few traces of accidental positive references to the capitalistic managerial classes, as a rationale for launching a full-scale rapprochement between General Motors and Mao Tse-Tung. That is to say, one leaves the book with the curious feeling that Boers would settle for a "dialogue with the world" in which Christianity says positive things inadvertently and, as it were, against its better judgment. (540)

Granted, then, that there is in fact an incipient universalism in the New Testament, just how significant is it in relation to the christological exclusivism? If there is no sense at all in which we can say that the text actually "intends" to present the original possibility of authentic existence, then it must be asked in what sense Ogden's fully existential approach can be termed *interpretation* /5/. If Boers's insight is sound, it must nevertheless be buttressed with a more fully developed hermeneutical method.

My project, then, is to test the usefulness of the Whiteheadian model by applying it to the problem of christology and anthropology in the New Testament. And my first step will be to investigate in depth a single christological witness and its concomitant soteriology on the basis of the hermeneutical perspective outlined in chapter 2. There are several complexes of material in the New Testament which would have served well as sounding boards for this question, but I have chosen the gospel of Matthew because I believe it is particularly relevant in two respects. First, both Ogden and Boers refer to Matt 25:31-46 in developing their arguments. More importantly, the Matthean gospel offers a striking combination of christological themes with a relatively undisturbed Jewish framework.

Although many scholars would take Matthew's positive attitude toward the Law as a sign of an inferior christology, there is another way of viewing the matter. There is no doubt that Matthew's orientation is very different from Paul's. But it is not beyond question that the difference disqualifies Matthew's gospel as a theology of grace (see Dodd,1953:57ff.; Davies, 1964:316ff.). It is at least arguable that the Matthean combination of christology and Law provides the clue for a theological conceptuality in which the Law-grace dichotomy is actually overcome. Gerhard von Rad has already taught us that in the Old Testament the Law functions *as* grace, although this insight has seldom been taken with full seriousness (388-409). If, then, it turns out to be the case that Matt 25:31-46 actually contains an incipient universalism, as Ogden claims, we have in Matthew the combination of a theology of grace with a soteriological scheme that overextends the christological witness. And such a combination would seem to offer serious challenge to the scholarly consensus that the exclusivist dimension of New Testament christology is an indispensable element in the message of the text.

I shall approach the Matthean gospel, then, with this question in mind: Which is the more basic element in the evangelist's witness? Is it his proclamation of the specific role of Jesus as the Christ in the economy of salvation or his statement of the quality of human existence that constitutes salvation—his christology or his anthropology? Keeping Käsemann's comments in mind, however, we must remember that we can hardly expect to find an explicitly anthropological formulation in the text. There is no question but that Matthew's own intention is in fact to witness to the salvation engendered by Jesus' mission as the Son of God. The subtler question, with which this study is concerned, is to what extent the salvation Jesus brings is actually tied to Jesus in a genuinely functional sense—i.e., to what extent Matthew actually carries through the implications of making Jesus the basis, as well as the bearer, of salvation. The question of christology and anthropology is thus to be sought in the more visible interaction between christology and soteriology. In inverted form, the question is to what extent Matthew might be said to present a soteriology that stands alone functionally, as a testimony to an "original possibility of authentic existence," apart from the christological framework within which Matthew has placed it.

Such a question is easily answered from the perspective of a purely descriptive or scientific exegesis: Matthew, without a doubt, ties salvation to Jesus. Whatever problems his correlation of soteriology and christology might entail, it is nevertheless his intention to make such a statement to his readers, and the interpreter's task is completed when that intention is uncovered. What I am asking in this investigation, however, is whether a process understanding of the language of the text might not place these anticipated problems in a different light and thus open up to the contemporary mind a dimension of the text not formerly accessible.

Matthew, of course, is but one of many witnesses in the New Testament. For that reason I shall seek to show, in a concluding chapter, how the question brought to Matthew might be raised in relation to some other portions of the New Testament and then to draw some conclusions about the nature of New Testament christology as a whole. But my initial task is to examine one christological formulation in detail.

NOTES

/1/ These alternatives, admittedly, are hardly exhaustive of the possibilites for interpreting New Testament christology. They are intended, though, to provide the limits within which a reading of that christology must be sought.

/2/ Ogden has nowhere stated his hermeneutical perspective explicitly, but the following quotations should show that he does in fact work on the basis of a stance similar to that which I am trying to develop systematically in this essay. "Part of the reason for this is my conviction that the Bible can be fittingly employed as the primary source and norm for a Christian understanding of existence only by recognizing that what finally counts as genuinely scriptural is not only what is *said* in the Bible or even what is *meant* there—although they, of course, are no more identical in the Bible than in any other written text!—but also what is necessarily *implied* by what the Bible means. . . . This is an example of what I take to be essential to a correct use of Scripture as the source and norm of theology. Without something like this, the Bible becomes little more than a series of prooftexts, with which one can establish virtually anything he pleases." (1977:151). See, further, n. /5/.

/3/ Braun's historical investigation, moreover, is irrelevant to the *systematic* question of whether authentic existence is in fact *possible* apart from the ministry of Jesus and the kerygma of the Church.

/4/ Against others who have tried to rehabilitate the distinction between possibility in principle and possibility in fact, it should be noted that Ogden's argument is not that this distinction is in and of itself meaningless but that it is illegitimate to use the term "possibility in principle" both to establish human responsibility *and* to deny the actual possibility of authentic existence apart from the Christian revelation: "For even if it was a 'possibility in principle' for them, it was *not* a 'possibility in fact'; and because it was not factually possible as an alternative to be resolved by their own free decision, it can hardly have been a possibility for which, in any meaningful sense, they were responsible" (1961:118). The point is that the distinction does not solve the question of responsibility. Thus Fenton's interpretation of "possibility in principle" as a possibility which "is not a phenomenon which contradicts human nature . . . a non-contradictory possibility, which is to say, something that can happen" (97) does no good. For it does not show how one can be held responsible for something simply because it is not contrary to human nature. Cf. also William O. Walker who, although accepting the distinction between "possibility in principle" and "possibility in fact," seems also to accept Ogden's arguments on responsibility.

/5/ It is instructive, in this connection, to note the position of Fritz Buri, who criticizes Bultmann regarding his understanding of the intention of New Testament language. Buri contends that the New Testament does not intend to present a self-understanding of the human person; it witnesses to an objective act of God and *on the basis of the objective reference offers a new self-understanding*. For the early believers it was the *event itself*—God's literally eschatological action—which was all-important: "What to us now appears as mythology is for [the early Christian] not the expression of a self-understanding; on the contrary, his self-understanding is based upon that mythical event which is presumed to be actual fact. So Bultmann inverts the relationship, since that eschatological mythology which was historicized into an imminent expectation—as he himself concedes—proved to be a delusion, while the Christian self-understanding, as Bultmann also shows, is in principle possible even without that mythology" (95). The New Testament message, according to Buri, is integrally related to a literal expection of the parousia. Thus when the parousia failed, the expectation failed, and even the self-understanding was called into question. But once we reverse the New Testament message, as Bultmann has actually done, and make the self-understanding primary, we deprive the Christ-event of its indispensability. In a way parallel to Ogden, then, Buri finds Bultmann's method inconsistent and opts for a position in which the self-understanding that accompanies the kerygma is given independent significance. But he differs from Ogden in this way: while Ogden, with Bultmann, claims to be true to the New Testament's own express emphasis, Buri frankly admits that he "reverses" that emphasis. It is important, however, to remember the sense in which Bultmann speaks of the "intention" of the New Testament: he does not mean the surface intention of the text, but the deeper intention disclosed by a content-criticism which plays off one aspect of the text against another. So it is useless to point to the New Testament's union of the mythological and the existential and consider Bultmann refuted; the real question is whether his "weighing" of various themes and modes of speech is convincing. Buri emphasizes a point Bultmann does not deny—that it is the modern world-view that leads to the observation of a discrepancy in the text. But insofar as Buri considers his own existential reading of the New Testament to be *interpretation* in any sense whatsoever, he is still standing upon Bultmannian ground. Whether he wishes to speak of his warrant as "intention" or not is not the real issue. What is really at stake, as Ogden has seen, is whether the presentation of the Christ-event is considered part of the mythology that has been joined to the existential witness. And at this point Buri's objection to Bultmann carries more weight. Whatever the "intention" of mythological language, it is illegitimate to brand all non-existential statements mythological and at the same time maintain that what amounts to an assertion about an exclusive act of God is not mythological. The matter can, I believe, be clarified considerably by a process hermeneutic which is able to distinguish between the author's own intention and the thought processes with which that author is engaged. When this distinction is recognized, the legitimacy of tracing the author's presuppositions is seen, and this insight provides the key to a deeper level of the text. (See, further, n. /2/.)

Part III

The Components of Matthew's Christology: Torah, Salvation, Grace

Nothing is more typical of Matthean scholarship than the characterization of the evangelist's christology as intimately bound to the notion of Law. However they are valued, one must inevitably deal with the designations of Jesus as one who "gives," "performs," "interprets," "upholds," or "revises" the Torah of Moses. Thus a crucial step in the present investigation is to determine precisely the way in which Jesus, the Torah he interprets, and the salvation he engenders, are related to one another. One objective of the next two chapters, then, will be to substantiate the following preliminary theses: 1) Matthew's soteriology is based upon Torah; while it is Jesus who brings salvation, by interpreting the Law, it is finally the Law itself that is the efficient means of salvation, and not any kind of vicarious atonement; 2) salvation, nevertheless, is not "legalistic," but actually rests upon a functional equivalent of the Pauline "grace."

The ultimate question, however, is how such statements—if they can be validated—are to be weighed in dealing with the question of an anthropological reading of Matthew's total christological scheme. It is at this point that the process methodology I have outlined will become explicitly operative. What I intend with respect to each thesis is first to approach a passage of determinative importance through a traditional exegesis and then to employ the insights of a process perspective at crucial points in order to evaluate the evidence in light of the broader concern I have expressed. In this way, I hope also to demonstrate the appropriateness of the Whiteheadian model to the actual linguistic form of the text.

Chapter 4

Torah and Salvation: Matt 5:17-20

17) Think not that I have come to abolish the law and the prophets; I have come not to abolish them but to fulfil them. 18) For truly, I say to you, till heaven and earth pass away, not an iota, not a dot, will pass from the law until all is accomplished. 19) Whoever then relaxes one of the least of these my commandments and teaches men so, shall be called least in the kingdom of heaven. 20) For I tell you, unless your righteousness exceeds that of the scribes and Pharisees, you will never enter the kingdom of heaven.

That Matt 5:17-20—the so-called introduction to the antitheses of the Sermon on the Mount—is a crucial passage in Matthew's total scheme may be demonstrated by an analysis of its place in the structure of chapters 5-7. The relationship of vs. 17 to vss. 21-48, the antitheses, is obvious: the latter give examples of the "fulfilled" Torah Jesus brings; they are specifications of the general statement regarding Jesus' relation to the demands of the Hebrew scriptures. What has seldom been seen, however, is that vs. 20 bears a relationship to 6:1-18 similar to that which vs. 17 bears to 5:21-48 /1/. Notice the term "scribes and Pharisees" in vs. 20 in comparison with its surrogate "hypocrites," which appears in each of the three sections regarding pious practice (almsgiving, 6:2; prayer, 6:5, fasting, 6:16), and the presence of "righteousness" in vs. 20 and in the beginning (6:1) of the triad. If 5:21-48 constitutes an exposition of the content of the "fulfilled" Torah, 6:1-18 presents concrete examples of the righteousness which "exceeds that of the scribes and Pharisees," mentioned in vs. 20. On the basis of this analysis, it may readily be seen that the material from 5:21 to 6:18 forms the core of the entire Sermon (Kürzinger). And the section in question, as the introduction to this core, is rather clearly Matthew's definitive theoretical statement on ethics, as well as his pronouncement on Jesus' relation to the Torah. It is, in fact, all-important for determining the way in which christology, soteriology, and Law interact in the Matthean gospel.

We may be doubly certain that Matthew is expressing a concern that is critical for him because of the highly composite nature of the literary unit. He seems to have taken vss. 18 and 19 from a section of Q (Schürmann; cf. Luke 16:14ff.) which has also supplied him with some of the other passages in the immediate context /2/. But vs. 20 cannot have been a part of this Q-context. Not only would it have been thematically out of place /3/, but it seems to be directed against proponents of strict observance while vs. 19 attacks antinomists. Nor can vs. 17 have been found in relation to vs. 18 either, since it is also thematically unsuited to the Q-context of Luke 16:14ff. /4/.

In addition, Matthew's editorial hand is clearly visible at several points: in the characteristically Matthean term διδάσκειν (to teach) in vs. 19, in the introductory and concluding elements in vs. 18 (ἕως [until]; ἕως · ἂν πάντα γένηται [until all is accomplished]), and in the ἀμὴν-formula (for, truly I say to you) imported into vs. 18 from the antitheses (Schürmann, 247f.).

Now if my analysis of the structure of the Sermon on the Mount is valid, then it is clear that Matthew wants to interpret vss. 18-19 in light of 17 and 20, and not vice-versa. For it is the latter, bracketing verses around which he has built the core of chapters 5-7. His emphasis thus cannot be upon literal obedience to the smallest command (vss. 18-19), but is rather upon the "fulfillment" of the Law (vs. 17) and the "higher righteousness" (vs. 20) demanded of Jesus' followers.

If vs. 20 is clear in its intention, the same can hardly be said of vs. 17, the interpretation of which hinges upon the difficult problem of the specific content of the verb πληροῦν(to fulfill). An understanding of this term is the key to the meaning of the entire passage. Edward P. Blair, following Ljungman's exhaustive treatment, classifies the suggested interpretations in the following way:

> 1) It is held that the word means "to do" or "to carry out": Jesus came not to abolish the law but to carry it out by obeying

it. . . . 2) To fulfill the law and the prophets is to reveal their true meaning, to give them a concise and final interpretation, to show their deepest intentions. . . . 3) The word means "to establish," "to validate," the law and the prophets. It stands here in opposition to the word "abolish." Jesus means to affirm the abiding validity of the word and the will of God. . . .What God has promised in the prophecies of the Scriptures he will perform.

[4]Ljungman objects to these interpretations and proposes a fourth position, which he derives in part from a study of a parallel saying in Matthew 3:15 . . . and also from the context of 5:17. He takes "righteousness" in 3:15 to mean not "acts of righteousness" or an ethical quality of goodness or uprightness but rather God's eschatological judgment of the wicked and salvation of the elect. Jesus knows that he has come to effect by his sacrificial death eschatological judgment and salvation. In his coming and through his work the will of God as expressed in the Scriptures is accomplished. (19; see also Ljungman: 19-36)

Each of these four suggestions merits detailed attention. Because, however, I believe the second and third are by far the more helpful, I will delay their treatment until after giving attention to the first and fourth.

1) Against the view that Jesus "fulfills" the Law through his own performance of its demands, it must be said that the context of the passage tends to discredit such a reading. The antitheses are instances of Jesus' interpretation of the Law, not of his own practices. There is no direct emphasis in the entire Sermon on the Mount on Jesus' own action with respect to the Law. Further, such an interpretation is best defended on the basis of a particular reading of the phrase, "until all is accomplished" ($\dot{\epsilon}\omega\varsigma$ $\dot{\alpha}\nu$ $\pi\dot{\alpha}\nu\tau\alpha$ $\gamma\acute{\epsilon}\nu\eta\tau\alpha\iota$) in vs. 18. The latter has frequently been interpreted as meaning "until Jesus has performed all the commandments," but Strecker has argued well against this. The reference cannot be to Jesus' action, "for this would contradict the unceasing validity of the Torah (vs. 18) and thus raise, once again, the problem of a temporal limit to this validity" (144; see also Schweizer).

Blair tries to justify reading $\pi\lambda\eta\rho o\hat{\nu}\nu$ as "to do," in the sense of performing the demands of the Law, on the basis of the term "righteousness," which occurs both at 5:20 and at 3:15. In the latter case, Jesus' baptism is justified by its necessity "to fulfill all righteousness." And Matthew does indeed use the term "righteousness" consistently to mean human action in conformity to God's will (Quell and Schrenk: 198). But that "righteousness" refers to Jesus' action in 3:15 does not necessarily mean that it refers to his obedience to the Torah as such. One might, for instance, emphasize the aspect of prophecy-fulfillment and see Jesus in the baptismal pericope as bringing to pass what God has intended, has announced through the prophets, and therefore demands of Jesus here as an act of obedience /5/. The emphasis would then be upon Jesus' role in salvation-history, rather than upon his performance of the Law. We need not, therefore, on account of 3:15, read into 5:17 a meaning not supported by the context.

4) As to Ljungman's alternate (and Paulinizing) reading of 5:17 in light of 3:15, neither the general New Testament usage apart from Paul nor the Matthean usage apart from these passages gives any basis for interpreting "righteousness" in terms of a forensic framework (Quell and Schrenk: 198 ff.). There may indeed be a rather intimate connection, for Matthew, between Jesus' baptism and his death. Surely the crucifixion is to be seen as an instance of his righteousness, and the reception of baptism functions similarly. But that Matthew has Jesus' death specifically in view in the phrase "to fulfill all righteousness" at 3:15 is not at all evident. Had he wanted to hold together the death and baptism themes in the way Ljungman imagines, it is incredible that he should have deleted from Mark the one phrase where this relationship is indisputably clear: "or to be baptized with the baptism with which I am baptized" (Mark 10:38d // Matt 20:22). However important the crucifixion may be for Matthew, Ljungman has failed to show that it creates a forensic righteousness.

A similar judgment must be passed against Fuchs's attempt to read the entire Sermon on the Mount in quasi-Pauline terms. Fuchs emphasizes that the instructions in the Sermon are issued to the Christian community as a polemic against the Jewish community per se (1960a:101-25, especially 107-109). This may be so, but one must ask by what right he moves from this assertion to the statement that the righteousness which is sought in the beatitudes is "the righteousness of Jesus Christ himself" (1960a:108). That righteousness may be "sought" and is therefore in some sense a gift does not imply a forensic interpretation. Given Matthew's general usage, which is clearly to refer to human conduct in harmony with God's will (cf. especially 5:20,6:1), the simplest way to understand such passages as 5:6 and 6:33 is as implying that God helps those who strive to act righteously to achieve the quality of existence they seek.

3) While the question of authenticity as a saying of Jesus has no importance in this connection, that of original meaning might. David Daube makes a good case for tracing the Greek πληροῦν to the Aramaic term *qyym* (to uphold). He contends that the background for the form of 5:17 is the rabbinic notion of an interpreter "upholding" the Torah by showing "that the text is in agreement with his teaching" (60). Supportive of Daube's contention is the fact that a Palestinian setting for the verses is quite likely, since it is here that Jesus' relation to the Torah would have been debated most sharply.

The interpretation of πληροῦν as "establish" or "uphold" is supported by Gerhard Barth. According to common linguistic usage, he notes, "to 'fulfill' . . . a word does not mean to modify or change its content, but to perform what the word says, bring it to actualization. . . ." From this observation Barth concludes that the best rendering of πληροῦν is "'establish' the law and the prophets" (69). And although he notes that Matthew's term has broader connotations than the Aramaic *qyym,* so that "the establishing of the law is by no means limited to Jesus' teaching" (69, n. 3), the primary reference is in fact to "Jesus' teaching, as it is worked out in 5:10ff." (69).

Ljungman raises an important question in relation to the assumed background of the term: "Does one not deprive [πληροῦν] of its point and its meaning if he brings in [*qyym*] and lets it govern the interpretation?" (31) In other words, why would Matthew choose "to fulfill" to render a term best translated as "to establish?" Why, for example, does he not choose ἱστάναι, which approximates the meaning of the Aramaic?

The possibility that Ljungman overlooks, however, is that the discrepancy in meaning between *qyym* and πληροῦν is evidence of Matthew's redactional creativity. It seems likely to me that Matthew has, with a change of nuance through translation and the overpowering weight of a supplied context, shaped the original saying to fit his conception of Jesus' relation to the Law. What Ljungman's argument discloses, then, is not the background but the foreground of the term. If Matthew chooses this term rather than the more obvious one to translate *qyym,* we must ask why this choice was made and how it alters the original sense of the material. We cannot be satisfied with a recovery of the original sense but must seek to determine the precise nuance of the Greek term in its present context.

And the context does in fact seem to demand a reading that involves understanding "fulfillment" in a way that is related to Jesus' teaching. Further, the juxtaposition of πληροῦν over against καταλύειν (to abolish) would indeed seem to confirm the specific notion of "upholding" or "establishing." In a way partially analogous to the practice of any rabbi, then, Jesus "upholds" the Law, in his teaching, by confirming its continuing validity. The context thus confirms the relevance of the Aramaic *qyym* to our problem, and Daube and Barth are to that extent justified in their renderings.

Barth is also correct, however, in hinting that the Greek term contains more than the original. A consideration of the phrase "until all is accomplished" in vs. 18 gives good reason to see in πληροῦν a nuance perhaps best captured through reference to the notion of "actualization." That the phrase in vs. 18 does not refer simply to the parousia is evident from the redundancy that would result from such an interpretation /6/. And, as already noted, it cannot refer to Jesus' own obedience to the Law. But it can, as Strecker contends, refer to the performance of the Law by the disciples and the later community: "The interpretation must after all be derived from the subsequent verses, which are directed at the disciples and the community (vs. 20!)" (104)/7/. Jesus "fulfills" the Law, in other words, by teaching his disciples in order that they might act upon that teaching and so bring the Law and the prophets to actualization. The righteousness of Christians—their obedience, engendered by Jesus' teaching—is in its own right the actualization of what God has both promised and demanded through the scriptures.

One may thus agree with Trilling (174) that fulfillment of the Law and the prophets in this passage suggests both a normative and a salvation-historical dimension. Jesus "establishes" and "actualizes" the Law and the prophets by teaching in such a way that both what God has promised through the prophets and what he has demanded through the Law are now realized: now is the time in which true righteousness will appear; the goal of God's continuing salvation-history—or at least its preliminary stage— is reached. Ljungman is quite justified, then, in using passages such as Josh 21:45 to interpret the words "until all is accomplished." The notion here is that the word "should not return until . . . God's whole will has been accomplished" (42).

Clearly, then, Matthew stands both in continuity and in discontinuity with Paul. Since it is in Jesus, God's envoy, that the Law and the prophets are fulfilled, the righteousness of the disciples may be seen as in some sense God's own accomplishment. It is indeed something that can be petitioned for! God, through his own activity, provides for, evokes that righteousness. And Jesus' abiding presence, promised in 28:20, surely in some way relates to the phrase about keeping the commandments that precedes it. Against Windisch (1951:128) it must therefore be said that there is indeed in the Sermon on the Mount an equivalent of the Pauline understanding of the Spirit. On the other hand, since the righteousness of which Matthew speaks is human action (and there appears to be no other way to read this term in 5:20, where it is understood as a matter of degrees) /8/, Windisch is still right in playing off Paul and the Sermon against one another. In our passage, God is seen as creating righteousness precisely in the Old Testament sense—by speaking, through a messenger, that Torah which calls his servants to him.

Now one question that has not been answered is why Matthew chooses πληροῦν, rather than ἱστάναι, to render *qyym*. But the answer is hopefully apparent. He intends more than the original contains. To begin with, he is interested in a salvation-historical nuance that might not come across in ἱστάναι. But there is another nuance that I believe is also present. It is best treated, however, in connection with the final suggestion for rendering the verb in 5:17.

2) The most significant argument against interpreting πληροῦν as "to sum up" or "to epitomize" is that this reading does not have clear support in the New Testament or other Greek literature. Walter Bauer does favor such a rendering in Gal 5:15, translating as follows: "the whole law has found its expression in a single word" (677). According to Burton, however, πληροῦν is "never used in the sense which this interpretation requires either in N.T., the LXX, or in any Greek writer so far observed" (295). Still, the root meaning of the term does not have to be pushed far to obtain this sense, and there is some reason to believe that Matthew pushes it in just this direction.

I begin by noting Strecker's contention that πληροῦν cannot mean "to establish" in the sense of simple, unqualified confirmation, since the Matthean form of the antitheses so clearly entails some sort of modification of the actual form of the Law (147) /9/. Jesus' right interpretation involves actual "changes" in the written code, for example, at 5:31ff., 38ff., and 43ff. Strecker is, I believe, essentially correct on this point, but there are two considerations that are of determinative importance in evaluating it.

First, the form of the antitheses is based upon a rabbinic model, as Daube has shown /10/. The rabbinic "but thou must say," which stands behind Matthew's "but I say unto you," involves the substitution of "a new, freer meaning for a literal rendering." The teachers of Jesus' time were not "unaware that exegesis might be tantamount to legislation" (59). It would thus be incorrect to assume that we are faced with the simple alternative between interpretation and legislation. Even for the rabbis interpretation could involve significant modification. Jesus' "abrogation" of some parts of the Law therefore need not contradict the contention that he "establishes" or "actualizes" the Torah. But Strecker is accurate in saying that Jesus' "actualization" of the Law is not *simple* confirmation.

Second, while Jesus' teaching entails modification of the written code, Matthew nevertheless asserts in vss. 18 and 19 that the whole of the Law remains. As Strecker himself notes, then, Matthew's view constitutes an antinomy: the Old Testament Law is valid, but some parts of it are invalid (146f.). And in two revisions of the Markan text Matthew reveals the principle by which the modification takes place. At 19:3-9 he rearranges the Markan debate on divorce (Mark 10:2-12) and in the process gives added emphasis to Mark's reference to the theme of creation. The resultant climactic clause at 19:8b, "but from the beginning it was not so," clearly identifies God's primordial will as the hermeneutical principle by which the Torah is to be interpreted. Then, at 22:40, he adds to the Markan pericope on the two great commandments (Mark 12:28-34) the comment that "on these two commandments depend all the law and the prophets," thus specifying the content of God's primordial will as love.

If, then, Jesus "actualizes" the Law by interpreting it in light of God's primordial love-command, the nuance of "summing up" would seem to be effectively present. There is, moreover, an abundance of evidence that the evangelist actually carries this hermeneutical principle through in a consistent and systematic fashion. To begin with, there is a special-Matthean passage loosely parallel to 22:40. At 7:12 Matthew concludes his Golden Rule (// Luke 6:31), which is itself a variant form of the second great commandment, with the phrase, "for this is the law and the prophets." In addition, he closes the antitheses with the pericope on perfect love (5:43-48), thus defining the "higher righteousness" of vs. 20 in terms of human love of the quality of God's own. At 23:23 (// Luke 11:42) he reworks a Q-passage in light of Mic 6:8, creating the impression that Jesus' rejection of the Pharisees' teaching is directed specifically to their failure to use the love-command as the central criterion for legal interpretation. Significantly, there are also hints that Matthew sees the conflict-stories as concretizations of Jesus' adherence to the love-principle. At 7:12 he inserts the scripture quotation, "I desire mercy and not sacrifice," which justifies Jesus' "illegal" Sabbath conduct both in 12:1-8 (// Mark 2:23-28) and 12:9-14 (// Mark 3:1-6). He also adds 12:11-12a, containing the hermeneutical comment, "so it is lawful to do good on the sabbath." Barth's summation seems justified: "Matthew knows very well how to draw the consequences from 22:40" (79).

So what, finally, does it mean for Matthew's Jesus to say that he has come to "fulfill" the Law and the prophets? It means that he "establishes" or "upholds" the Torah by interpreting it definitively on the basis of God's primordial will, which is epitomized in the dual command to love. He thus both confirms its abiding validity and modifies its actual form. And his definitive interpretation becomes the basis for a new obedience, the higher righteousness, which leads to salvation. Jesus thus "actualizes" God's plan of salvation-history, promised in the scriptures as a whole, precisely by facilitating that genuine righteousness which defines the life of the Kingdom.

On the basis of this understanding of 5:17-20, it would now seem possible to give tentative approval to my first thesis: the rightly-interpreted Torah would indeed seem to be the actual basis of salvation. For it is precisely Jesus' definitive rendering of the Law that brings about that genuine righteousness that God demands. If an atonement theology is operative in the gospel, it has not yet appeared, and there would seem to be little place for it. There are, to be sure, certain passages that could be quoted in support of such an emphasis, and I will deal with them in time. But 5:17-20 would seem to point in quite another direction.

It is equally clear, however, that Jesus himself plays a crucial role in the process of salvation. It is he, after all, who issues the definitive interpretation of the Torah, and the word ἦλθον (I have come) in vs. 17 is clearly an expression of Jesus' messianic status. Moreover, it is clear that the authority by which Jesus speaks (28:18) is God's own authority. But if my treatment of 5:17-20 is valid, Jesus' salvific function nevertheless consists precisely in his appearance at the apex of salvation-history (see ahead, chapter 9) as God's unique representative who issues the Torah that facilitates salvation.

At this point a crucial question arises. If Jesus issues the command that engenders obedience, does this imply that obedience was not really possible beforehand, that Jesus *creates the possibility* of righteousness—if not through his atoning death, then through the simple giving of the Law? Taken in isolation, 5:17-20 might seem amenable to such a logical projection. But it must be said that Matthew himself does not seem to interpret Jesus' engendering of obedience as making possible what was formerly impossible. The implication of 19:8b is that Israel should have known what God's will regarding divorce really is, despite Moses' concession to the peoples' hardness of heart /11/. And the entire controversy with the scribes and Pharisees and all the judgments against Israel's earlier failure to repent (cf., e.g., 21:33-36) clearly presuppose that the ethic of the Kingdom was available all along and that therefore all those who rejected it are responsible for not having obeyed it. What is the sense of the indictment at 23:23, "these you ought to have done, without neglecting the others," apart from such an assumption?

The telling point, though, is Matthew's revision of the pericope regarding the right use of parables (13:10-17 // Mark 4:10-12). For by substituting ὅτι (because) for ἵνα (so that) in vs. 13, he neatly avoids the deterministic implications of the Markan text. Jesus speaks in parables as a result of the people's misperceptions, not as a way of obstructing perception. The situation here has to do with Jesus' ministry and not Israel's past failure, but the point in either case is the same. Matthew wants it understood that Israel had many chances to repent.

Matthew does not, of course, state explicitly the point I am stressing; he consistently reveals, however, that he is assuming it. So the case might best be stated this way: There is no reason to suppose that Matthew sees Jesus' preaching as fostering an ethic made possible by Jesus' appearance when the gospel reveals such a concern to establish Israel's guilt and concomitant responsibility (see Hummel:158). He consistently assumes that Jesus preached an ethic which, while defining the life of the Kingdom, was valid apart from both the imminence of the Kingdom and Jesus' own presence as its herald.

Still, it may be asked whether Matthew might not view the matter in a paradoxical fashion. Does he perhaps simply hold together the notions of Israel's culpability and the factual impossibility of righteousness prior to Jesus on the other? To establish this one would have to show that the evangelist sees no actualization of obedience before the advent of Jesus—hardly a likely possibility for one with an appreciation of salvation history such as Matthew's. And the fact is that he does not really indicate in any way, as far as I can see, that he thinks of the time prior to Jesus as characterized by the kind of cosmic corruption that renders obedience factually impossible (see ahead, chapter 9).

What we do have to reckon with, though, is Matthew's belief in the *facticity* of sin in Israel's history. Jesus' heralding of the eschatological occasion for repentance and his "fulfillment" of the Law thus in one sense create a new situation by exposing a possibility for existence that is largely unrealized. The assumption of this newness is juxtaposed over against the relentless assertion of human responsibility prior to Jesus, but the precise relationship between the two themes is never explicitly addressed. Thus it is necessary to acknowledge a certain imprecision or tension in Matthew's thought at this point—although not a genuine paradox, since he does not proclaim all humanity to be under the power of sin as does Paul (Rom 3:9).

It is conceivable, of course, that Matthew takes a different view with respect to his own time in history. If he does not see Jesus as making possible what was formerly impossible, he might nevertheless deny the *present* possibility of righteousness outside the Christian community. Such a possibility, however, can be evaluated only on the basis of a study of Matthew's ecclesiology and eschatology. And that is a task I will pursue later in the study. The questions of immediate relevance at this point are whether a process model of language is in any way confirmed by the investigation up to this point and whether that model is of any help in assessing the preliminary results.

A process hermeneutic, as I have defined it, begins with a recognition of the bifocal character of the language of a text: it is, on the one hand, fragmentary and imprecise; it has, on the other hand, a metaphysical thrust which may function in a way that is quite at odds with a univocal rendering of its terms. I begin, then, by noting two points in the material examined at which the fragmentary and imprecise character of the language appears in exaggerated fashion. First, as was noted earlier, Matthew's doctrine of Torah is stated as an antinomy: the whole law remains valid; some parts of it are abrogated. And the fact that the love-command embodies the whole does not really remove the problem, for 5:18 speaks of the perpetuation of every iota and dot. Matthew, as we have seen, has every intention of circumventing some dots and iotas himself. But he allows the statement to stand in its rigid form while in effect qualifying it by other elements in his text. So the point is that his language fails to express his meaning in univocal fashion. To say everything he wants to say, he must set contradictory statements side by side. (The fact that the rabbis, too, could speak of "revision" as "interpretation" does not remove the logical problem.) Language fails him again in his attempt to juxtapose the novelty of Jesus' revised Torah with his insistence on a voluntaristic view of human nature. Jesus' message does foster a new obedience, but it is just that obedience that was expected—and therefore deemed possible!—all along. As I have said, Matthew avoids paradox here through his consistent assertion of universal responsibility. But he does not find the words to render his juxtaposition fully intelligible.

The fragmentary character of language is easy enough to demonstrate in almost any text, and all the more so in an ancient religious one. The crucial contribution of a process hermeneutic will lie in what it can say beyond this. Do we, then, have evidence of a metaphysical thrust in the material so far considered? This is a question that is best answered in conjunction with an explicit process analysis of the passage in question.

Since any linguistic formulation is actually an imperfect attempt to state propositions, which are primarily lures for feelings, a helpful first step should be to identify the major lures at work in the passage and thus give a better perspective on what is actually signified. If the reader of the text—as seems evident—is the intended prehending subject of the propositions, toward what does the language of the text direct the reader's attention? Four basic lures seem readily identifiable. 1) A major "non-linguistic factor" is, of course, the author's assumption of the Christian commitment itself. Matthew's gospel is written for Christian consumption. Thus when Jesus in vs. 17 uses the messianic term ἦλθον (I have come), we must recognize a subtle lure toward the apprehension of and recommitment to Jesus as Messiah, and in this context that means principally as authoritative interpreter of the Torah. 2) Beyond this, however, the complex of vss. 17-19 draws the reader toward a recognition of the abiding validity of the Torah itself as the means of entering the Kingdom. 3) Vs. 20 fosters a negative apprehension of the Pharisees as exemplifying the wrong approach to righteousness and the Kingdom. 4) But then the same verse both draws upon the preceding verses and looks forward to the antitheses in order to lure the reader toward a desire for the "higher righteousness" which is delineated by Jesus' definitive interpretation of the Torah.

This much is, I believe, readily discernible in the linguistic formulations of the present text itself. But if we push beyond that immediate level and ask about less evident presuppositions, then it becomes apparent that one major presupposition underlies the entire complex. In raising the question of Torah at all, Matthew reveals that he is working within the context of a Jewish-Christian salvation-history. In the background stands the assumption of God's continuing history of self-revelation to his people Israel. Thus in luring the reader to a recognition of Jesus and an understanding of his specific relation to Torah, Matthew also presents 5) a lure toward recognition of and recommitment to the God whom Jesus represents. And this lure brings with it a .corollary truth-claim: Jesus does in fact represent the God revealed in Israel's history, and that God is in fact at work in the world. So there is at least one lure present in this text that has cosmic proportions; it implies something about the nature of the universe—i.e., that it is the arena of the action of a gracious and omnipotent deity.

This lure, however, is neatly bound in by its confessional grounding. The God whose activity is assumed here is discernible not in human experience per se but only in a special history of revelation. But if I am correct in identifying Jesus' interpretive principle, which lies behind his "fulfillment" of the Law and his presentation of a higher righteousness, then the passage in question also contains 6) an indirect lure toward recognition of the love-command as the key to the Torah which brings salvation. In calling his followers to himself and to his/God's Torah, Jesus also calls them to a discernment of God's *will* as the demand for love. This is an insight that must be considered carefully.

There is an obvious sense in which this indirect lure has a universalistic, as opposed to a confessional, character. Unlike the calls to Jesus, Torah, and the God of Israel's history, the call to love *can* be stated in a universalistic way—i.e., as an invitation to the recognition of a principle that is perceptible by human beings per se, simply by virtue of their participation in existence in the world. Matthew, of course, does not actually state the lure in that way. He does not, in fact, state it at all, but merely implies it. And he implies it by means of statements that are obviously confessional in orientation. Nevertheless, the fact remains that the love-command is in principle abstractable from its confessional context. So the question arises: Does Matthew tie this love-principle so tightly to the confessional scheme through which it is recognized that its functioning is inseparable from the confession, or does that principle actually *ground* the confession, so that the love-standard per se takes on an independent soteriological significance?

This is by no means an easy question to answer. The fact that one aspect of Matthew's soteriological scheme is logically separable from another aspect is in my estimation of no small import. But one must allow the evangelist to insist upon whatever connections he will. Still, if our ultimate goal is not simply the author's intention, but the total thought-complex with which he is involved, we must—as Bultmann well knew—take a critical stance. What I suggest, then, is a rephrasing of our question in this way: Does the author himself betray in any way that this lure actually *functions* in his thought-scheme as an independent ground of the confession, whatever the witness he might consciously *intend* to make?

Even this question is not answered so easily. But I believe there are subtle hints that the lure toward the love-standard does actually transcend the confessional lures in a functional sense in Matthew's thinking process. One of these hints occurs in the immediate context of the passage—in the sixth antithesis, Matt 5:44-48, the inclusion of which in the series is undoubtedly due to Matthew's own hand (see n. /9/). C. H. Dodd has treated this passage in his article, "Natural Law in the Bible," identifying it as one of several passages which transcend covenantal thought by appealing to experience per se as the ground of a particular religious insight. A genuinely universalistic thrust is apparent in vs. 45b: one must love one's enemies because God himself "makes his sun rise on the evil and on the good, and sends rain on the just and on the unjust." The appeal is not to Jesus' presence or even to the Torah or the history of Israel, but to an order of creation perceptible in nature itself and therefore, by implication, available to all persons in all times and places. As Matthew's Jesus explicates his Torah, then, he actually transcends the appeal to God's Torah precisely by reference to the love-principle, perceptible through experience in the world per se, *as a way of recognizing the validity of the Law's command*. The undeniable implication is that the love-principle actually grounds and validates the Torah, rather than vice-versa, and so has a significance of its own, independent of its covenantal context.

One may ask, of course, whether Matthew even notices the implications of this passage and whether he does not vitiate its non-covenantal force by placing it in the eschatological context of the Sermon on the Mount. There is no question but that the Sermon represents the ethic of the Kingdom for Matthew. But, as Windisch shows, it bears none of the marks of an interim ethic, such as that of I Cor 7 (1951:30). For in no instance in Matthew is it apparent that the content of obedience to God's will is determined by the imminence of the Kingdom. In 4:17, for instance, an eschatological warning is given so as to intensify the call to obedience, but without any hint that the demand is inherently related to the situation of imminence—i.e., that anything less or different would be required were the Kingdom not so close. The same may be said with respect to the parables of the Kingdom in Matt 13 and the apocalyptic warnings in Matt 24-25. Obedience becomes a more crucial issue, but the content of God's demand does not seem to change. So the eschatological context of 5:44-48 says nothing with respect to its universalistic force.

As to whether Matthew notices the universalistic implications of the passage, it must be said that there is nothing in the context to prove that he does. But that is not, from a process perspective, the important question. What must be asked, rather, is whether he allows these implications to function in a meaningful way in the remainder of the gospel. So the real question is whether 5:45b is paralleled by other passages in Matthew, and that is the question to which I will address myself in part 4.

But it is relevant at this point to recall a passage already mentioned—19:3-9 (// Mark 10:2-12)—and to subject it to a more detailed analysis. Dodd includes this passage among his examples of "natural law," pointing first to vss. 4f.: "Have you not read that he who made them from the beginning made them male and female, and said, 'For this reason a man shall leave his father and mother and be joined to his wife. . . ?'" Although the saying is found in the Torah, "the intention seems to be to base the maxim on the *fact* recorded in Genesis—'male and female created he them'"(55)/12/. Although the universalistic force is present in Mark's version, it should be noted that Matthew's revision preserves that force while providing a more direct reference to God ("he who made them"). And, in any case, the emphasis is heightened by Matthew's repetition of the creation theme in 19:8b—"but from the beginning it was not so"—which results in a more direct confrontation of Moses' "concession" (see Hummel:50) and has the added effect of bracketing Jesus' reply with the creation motif.

While this passage does not make direct reference to the love-standard, it does quite clearly indicate in a formal way Jesus' hermeneutical principle: the Torah is to be interpreted precisely in light of God's *primordial* will which stands behind it. Insofar, then, as Matthew explicitly identifies that will with the dual command to love, we have here a parallel to 5:45b. Matthew once again allows Jesus to appeal directly to the structure of reality when interpreting the Torah. It is true that the structure indicated in this passage is recorded in the Torah and that, as Hummel notes (50), Matthew here views God's primordial will as expressing the deepest intention *of* the Torah, not as something set against it. But that does not alter the fact that the appeal implicitly transcends Torah as such, since Matthew invokes God's act of creation, not the Torah's statement of a command, as implying his standard of righteousness.

It is important, however, to note the continuation of Jesus' reply in 19:9: "And I say to you. . . ." It is Jesus' own reading of the Law's deepest intention that is contrasted to Moses' concession. If, then, at numerous points Matthew replaces references to Moses with references to God (Mark 10:7 // Matt 15:4; Mark 12:26 // Matt 22:31), his purpose is to set Jesus above Moses as representing God more directly (Kingsbury 1975:91). So in the present passage we have to reckon with a strong christological lure also. But we must remember that Jesus' status as God's unique representative is defined precisely in terms of his place in history as the one who brings the primordial/eschatological Torah. So the christological lure does not constitute a critique of Torah-soteriology but only of the "old" approrach to Torah, that represented by Jesus' critics. And to the extent that the universalistic lure transcends the appeal to Torah it transcends the christological witness also.

What, then, is the result of this somewhat intricate analysis? It would seem that there are in fact subtle points at which universalistic lures seem to function in Matthew's gospel. But these lures, it must be admitted, are present only obliquely in the material so far considered. So the question remains whether a universalistic emphasis appears less ambiguously at other points.

But if the extra-confessional lure in Matthew can be further substantiated, then some far-reaching conclusions can be drawn regarding Matt 5:17-20. Let us recall the two points of tension in Matthew's thought mentioned earlier—the antinomy constituted by his doctrine of the "fulfillment" of the Torah and the milder tension (or imprecision) constituted by the juxtaposition of Jesus' role as the one who engenders obedience with the universality of human responsibility. One must ask in the former case whether the interpreter must be satisfied with the notation that Matthew's doctrine of Torah does not make full logical sense. Such a recognition is perhaps as far as a purely descriptive exegesis can go. But a process analysis poses another possibility. Matthew's concern for the abiding validity of the Torah is part and parcel of his commitment to a scheme of salvation-history. He is concerned for the ongoing significance of the Law because he believes that Jesus is in fact the fulfillment of a preliminary revelation given to Israel. Insofar as he speaks of Jesus as fulfilling the Law and the prophets he speaks in covenantal language. The universalistic lure which lurks in the background of our passage, however, transcends covenantal thought by appealing to universally perceptible notions. It thus by nature constitutes a subtle critique of covenantal thought per se. So its very presence raises the question as to the actual centrality and indispensability of the salvation-history which appears on the surface to be so crucial to Matthew's thought-patterns. Perhaps, then, the ultimately functional idea in 5:17-20 is not that Jesus fulfills the Law and the prophets, but simply that he expresses God's will. Perhaps the real function of Matthew's antinomy—which is to be distinguished from his conscious purpose in presenting it—is to create, through imprecision, a tension that actually draws the reader beyond the univocal meanings of the terms "Torah" and "fulfill" to an apprehension of something else—Jesus' role as bearer of God's *primordial* will, universally perceptible.

In a similar way, if it turns out to be the universalistic reference that is the more basic element, then Matthew's assertion of Jesus' engendering of obedience must be interpreted in such a way as to do no violence to his assertion of human responsibility, for the latter theme is a correlate of the universalistic lure. In this case, I believe a traditional exegesis must come to the same conclusion. But a process analysis strengthens the insight and explains how the highly imprecise assertion of Jesus' role actually opens into the broader reference. From such a perspective it is only to be expected that the confessional witness will be stated in an elliptical fashion that will stand in some tension with that to which it ultimately refers. What may be important, then, is not that Jesus presents a literally new possibility, but that the possibility he presents is in fact God's own primordial will for human beings. The assertion of newness, in other words, need not be taken univocally; it may, rather, be a sign that Jesus' teachings stand over against the inauthentic possibilities to which people are *generally* accustomed. In doing so, these teachings would represent that authentic possibility for which God has always held humanity responsible, precisely because it is the authentic human possibility.

The universalistic lure, then, if it can be substantiated as a significant element in the thought processes with which Matthew is engaged, can be appreciated in such a way as to lead the interpreter through certain tensions in the text. But it does so by calling into question a univocal reading of all the confessional elements in the proximate lures, precisely because it transcends confessional limits and stands as the logical ground of less inclusive references. The proximate lures cannot be severed from the truth-claims they entail, for a process analysis demands that their conceptual import be taken seriously. But when interpreted in light of a universalistic reference, those truth-claims undergo a shift in locus.

Just what value would be assigned to the christological witness by this interpretation is a matter that I will discuss in parts 4 and 6. This reading of 5:17-20 is in any case put forth at this juncture more as a question than as a claim, since the universalistic lure is present only obliquely here. Hopefully, however, this analysis has served to demonstrate the "appropriateness" of the Whiteheadian model to the language of the Matthean gospel and as a helpful tool in approaching the broader problem under consideration. If my exegesis of 5:17-20 lends support to the thesis that Matthew's soteriology rests functionally upon Torah, a process analysis raises the question as to whether Matthew's obvious christological interest is not in some sense transcended and interpreted by a soteriology that is functionally independent of it.

Chapter 5

Torah as Grace: Matt 11:25-30

> 25) At that time Jesus declared, "I thank thee, father, Lord of heaven and earth, that thou hast hidden these things from the wise and understanding and revealed them to babes; 26) yea, Father, for such was thy gracious will. 27) All things have been delivered to me by my Father; and no one knows the Son except the Father, and no one knows the Father except the Son and any one to whom the Son chooses to reveal him. 28) Come to me, all who labor and are heavy laden, and I will give you rest. 29) Take my yoke upon you, and learn from me; for I am gentle and lowly in heart, and you will find rest in your souls. 30) For my yoke is easy, and my burden is light."

An important question that arises out of the characterization of Matthew's soteriology presented in the preceding chapter is this: If Matthew finally ties salvation to Torah, is his christology then simply an aberration as viewed against the background of other New Testament witnesses? More specifically, is Matthew a "legalist," whose perspective is fundamentally different from that of Paul, John, and Jesus himself? Does a study of his christology and soteriology therefore have little value for a solution to the larger problem of the meaning of New Testament christology as a whole?

I will reserve a comparison of Matthew's christology to those of other segments of the New Testament until chapter 10. It is important, however, to address the question of Matthew's "legalism" at this point in order to avoid a misinterpretation of the contention that his soteriology is linked to Torah. A preliminary indication of Matthew's concept of "grace" has already appeared in the fact that Jesus' teaching does engender obedience. But, as we have seen, Matthew's emphasis falls upon human responsibility, so that the question of "self-salvation" is still pertinent. In this connection, Matt 11:25-30 is of great importance, for it exposes the way in which the command of the Torah is itself a functional equivalent of the Pauline notion of "grace." The passage is a major piece of evidence, in other words, for the second preliminary thesis indicated at the beginning of this chapter. On the other hand, it contains elements that might be interpreted in such a way as to place Matthew's emphasis upon Torah in a different light and call into question the importance of the extra-confessional elements of Matthew's thought. The passage thus provides an opportunity to subject some of my tentative conclusions to an early scrutiny while seeking to establish my second thesis.

If the ultimate origin of the materials present in this passage remains a matter of dispute (see Betz), there is nevertheless something approaching unanimity among recent interpreters regarding the role of the passage in its Matthean context. De Kruijf has argued convincingly that the revelation motif in these verses has to do with the secret of the Kingdom which is appearing in Jesus' ministry (65ff.) /13/. The element of secrecy here is of course quite different from the Markan "messianic secret" which Jesus himself maintains. For the emphasis in Matthew is not upon Jesus' intention to remain incognito but upon the inability of his enemies to grasp the significance of his ministry. The passage relates to its context primarily through the dual theme of Jesus' rejection by the Pharisees and acceptance by his disciples. The narrative section beginning at 11:1 is unified by the rejection theme, and Jesus' "easy yoke" stands as the antithesis of the Pharisaic attitude condemned through the negative examples of chapter twelve. The Pharisees cannot understand Jesus' ministry because of their hardness of heart, their refusal to see the Messiah in this humble man who challenges their claim upon the Kingdom. This basic understanding of the passage is widely accepted, but here the agreement ends.

Gerhard Barth sees Jesus' atoning death in the background. The "rest" ($\alpha\nu\alpha\pi\alpha\upsilon\sigma\iota\varsigma$) which Jesus offers the heavy laden is, according to Barth, grounded in Jesus' act in behalf of sinners:

> Jesus shows himself to be $\pi\rho\alpha\upsilon\varsigma$ [gentle] in that he, as the Messianic judge of the world, enters the ranks of sinners, submits to baptism and so, on behalf of sinners goes the way of

the cross. The yoke of Jesus is easy and light because Jesus acts for sinners, because the yoke of Jesus does not throw a man upon his own efforts but rather brings him into fellowship with the πραΰς. (148, n. 2; see also J. B. Bauer)

The problem with this view, however, is that there is nothing in the passage itself or its immediate context to suggest such a reading. One must import the atonement motif from 21:28 and 26:28, when the author himself does nothing to indicate that connection. Thus Strecker disputes Barth's interpretation and emphasizes the continuity between this passage and Matthew's notion of Jesus' intensification of the demands of the Law. The terms πραυς and ταπεινός (lowly), he notes, have an ethical reference. To take Jesus' yoke means to accept his standard of righteousness which is "easy" and "light" not because Jesus himself accomplishes the righteousness but because it leads ultimately to "rest:"

> Because the law of Christ, in contrast to the Pharisaic precepts, leads to "rest," it can be called χρηστός, [easy] even though it is more difficult in terms of its content; and insofar as the "yoke" of Jesus provides even now the ἀνάπαυσις [rest], it is termed "light," even though its demands are heavier. Ethical demand and eschatological gift therefore.accord with one another—but not in the sense that the latter assumes the former as a prerequisite or even less that, conversely, the "gift" precedes the "demand." To the contrary, the gift of salvation is present in Jesus' demand; the imperative itself has salvific significance. (174; see also Lambert)

Hans-Dieter Betz has challenged both Barth and Strecker, offering an interpretation which relates the present passage to 28:16-20 and 25:31-46. Betz sees the source of the "rest" not in the simple giving of the command itself, but in the risen Jesus' presence with his disciples at 28:20. And he finds this same indication of Jesus' presence in the Description of the Last Judgment (25:31-46), where it is again combined with Matthew's ethical interest. In the latter passage, Betz argues,

the Risen Lord is present in a mysterious way in "the least of
these my brothers," and it is in connection with this that the
words [learn from me, for I am gentle] have their validity. (24)

Thus in 11:25-30 the command to receive Jesus' yoke is a
command to imitate the action of the righteous who in the
judgment pericope minister to the lowly in whom Jesus is present.
And the contrast between Jesus' attitude toward the Law and that
of the Pharisees is to be seen in light of the theme of the "great
surprise" in that same passage:

> It is an easy yoke and a light burden because they do not
> "know"—the righteous no more than the unrighteous, for the
> man on the "path of righteousness" is not one to compute his
> reward or consider what he deserves. (24)

Now Betz's latter contention has real force. The context of
11:25-30 does indeed show that Jesus' attitude toward the Law is
to be contrasted to the meticulous calculations of the Pharisees.
By centering upon the sole valid criterion for ethical activity—the
dual command to love, here expressed in the terms "gentle" and
"lowly"—the follower of Jesus is able to meet situations with the
same simplicity and spontaneity which Jesus exhibits in his
encounters with Pharisees in the passages that follow. Whether or
not the theme of surprise is directly in view here is not ultimately
important; the force of the ethic of the passage is the contrast to
the Pharisaic "burdens."

On the other hand, Strecker would seem to be correct at two
points. First, the "easiness" of the ethic is indeed compatible with
Jesus' intensification of the demands of the Law. The
commandment is easier by virtue of its simplicity; it is harder
because it demands a genuine, total obedience to God's will rather
than external compliance with definable rules. Second,
Strecker is surely correct in speaking of a genuine unity between
indicative and imperative. But in order to appreciate this latter
point it is best to consider first Betz's contention that the
indicative issues not from the command itself but from Jesus'
presence.

In the first place, Jesus' presence at 28:16-20 is something quite different from his identification with the suffering ones at 25:31-46. If my reading of the latter passage is correct (see below, chapter 7), Jesus makes himself one with all suffering humanity. At 28:16-20, however, Jesus promises his presence to the body of disciples to empower them to keep the love-commandments and to foster the mission of the Church. It cannot be maintained that the righteous who minister to the needy at 25:31-46 are enabled to do so by the power of Jesus' presence, for Jesus is present in the *needy*. And he is present in such a way that the revelation of his unity with them is a surprise to the righteous. The judgment scene thus presents a view quite at odds with Betz's reading. Here the indicative and the imperative are clearly inseparable. The problem of enabling power is not in view at all; the possibility of doing the just deed is assumed as a matter of course.

But in that at 28:16-20 the life of the Church is expressly brought under the aegis of Jesus' empowering presence, the question is whether 11:25-30 is to be interpreted in this light. And there is reason to believe that it is. For 11:28 seems to constitute a promise that those who follow Jesus will be given the power to obey his commandments. But does this promise mean what Betz thinks it means? I must insist that there is no hint of mystical or quasi-mystical indwelling. For the "coming" to Jesus commanded in vs. 28 is defined in this way in vs. 29: "take my yoke upon you and learn from me." The ultimate reference is to Jesus' yoke, his commandment, which he of course exemplifies in that he himself is "gentle" and "lowly." It is the taking of Jesus' yoke, the "learning" of his commandments which leads to "rest," and it is this yoke again which is described as "easy." It is thus the yoke itself which Jesus offers as the agent of grace. The imperative, as Strecker argues, is itself sufficient indicative.

Now of course Jesus himself is the one who delivers the revelation from God and who says "come to me" and "learn from me" and who relates the yoke to his own gentleness and lowliness of heart. But it would be false to claim on this basis that the present passage envisions Jesus' presence as somehow prior to and independent of his call to obedience, that the indicative grounds the imperative. The weight of Matthew's unabashed ethical interest and the plain sense of vs. 30 point to another conclusion:

> Matthew distinguishes formally between κηρύσσειν [to preach] and διδάσκειν [to teach], but not in terms of content; didache possesses kerygmatic character just as, conversely, kerygma possesses didactic character. . . .If the preaching of Jesus is to be understood as an essentially ethical demand, kerygma and didache cannot in fact be separated in terms of content. . . .It is not that teaching contains the "execution" or "definition" of a prior "indicative" kerygma: the imperative is identical with the indicative. (Strecker: 175)

If this is true, however, then we must take a second look at 28:16-20. If Matthew's consistent view entails the unity of indicative and imperative, it is unlikely that his notion of Jesus' empowering presence is here understood in a way that contradicts this view. And, as a matter of fact, it is perfectly in line with the sense of 28:16-20 (and also with 18:20) to understand Jesus' presence in the community as a surrogate for his original presence as the authoritative interpreter of the Torah. In other words, the grace constituted by Jesus' presence in the community is of similar nature to that constituted by his stating of the will of God. Just as Jesus' teaching calls and enables the people to do what they should and therefore could have done apart from him, so now Jesus' presence in the community calls and enables his followers to obey the teachings they already possess. As in 11:25-30, Jesus is in the midst of his followers as the one who commands the "easy" yoke of love and *thereby* engenders true obedience. But to engender obedience, as we have seen, is not necessarily to create a wholly new possibility.

So the interesting result of our discussion is this: Matthew does embrace a strong notion of "grace," but this "grace" seems to issue not from any kind of vicarious sacrifice, or even from Jesus' mystical presence, but rather from Torah itself—and, of course, from Jesus himself in the sense that he gives the definitive interpretation of the Law and abides with his people so that they may continually be confronted with its grace/demand and (18:20) work out its implications for their lives.

An analysis of 11:25-30, then, confirms my second thesis and does so in such a way as to lend strength to the first thesis also. But there are two elements in the passage that might seem to do violence to my conclusions in the preceding chapter. The first of these is seen in the way in which the evangelist has shaped the Wisdom material at his disposal in Q—a theme that Jack Suggs has treated in detail. What Suggs argues, in brief, is that Matthew's editing of this material reveals that for the evangelist Jesus assumes the function of Wisdom, which in Jewish tradition has already been identified with Torah. In the Q material, Jesus appears as the *representative* of Wisdom—the last and greatest of her envoys—but in Matthew Jesus *is* Wisdom and therefore *is* Torah. Quite obviously, an identification of Jesus with Torah would alter the significance of evidence that salvation is based upon Torah, so an evaluation of Sugg's work is crucial to my own project.

The evidence is impressive. Drawing upon the earlier work of James Robinson (1971), Suggs argues convincingly that Q contains a strain of Wisdom speculation in which Jesus, along with John the Baptist, appears as the envoy of Wisdom, one who transmits a revealed truth, rather than the unique savior whose vicarious suffering effects salvation (9). He then examines Matthew's editing of several Wisdom-oriented passages from Q with the following results.

1) At 11:19 (// Luke 7:35) Matthew has changed the saying on Wisdom's "children" to read "wisdom is justified by her deeds." This, Suggs argues, indicates that Matthew has in mind the "messianic deeds" of Jesus which are central in the section constituted by 11:2-24. From this he concludes that Matthew wants specifically *"to identify Jesus with Wisdom.* In this way, Jesus is no longer the last and greatest of Wisdom's children; in him are the deeds of Wisdom to be *uniquely* seen" (57). 2) Accordingly, the evangelist has inserted 11:12-15 into the Q context in order to reinforce this emphasis upon uniqueness:

"with John the Baptist the 'new' has erupted into history. John stands at a dividing point; the fulfillment of prophecy sets in with him" (57f.). 3) At 23:34 (// Luke 11:49) Matthew actually puts Wisdom's saying (Therefore I sent [will send] you [them] prophets . . .") into Jesus' mouth. He thus assigns to Jesus "a function which belongs to no figure in pre-Christian Judaism except Wisdom and God . . ." (59).

With respect to 11:25-30, Suggs argues that vss. 25-27 are a fragment of a hymn, preserved in Q, which belongs thematically to the world of Wisdom-speculation represented best in the Wisdom of Solomon and also in the Qumran writings (90-92, citing Davies, 1953). In each of these settings the election motif of Deutero-Isaiah has focused upon an individual, one who has "knowledge" of God, speaks of himself as a "child" of God, and terms God his father. The theme of the righteous one's rejection is also present in the parallels. Nevertheless, Suggs writes,

> it would be a serious mistake to regard the afflictions of the Qumran psalmist(s) and those of the righteous Son in the Wisdom of Solomon as being redemptive for others or even as being a part of the revelation the prophets mediate. (95)

That the rightous one is vindicated means only that the truth of his teaching is confirmed; it has nothing to do with a vicarious atonement. In the Q hymn, the typical figure is identified with a historical person—Jesus. But the thought-mode is not otherwise disturbed.

When these verses are placed into Matthew's context, however, they acquire a new meaning. First, "these things" that are "revealed to babes" now logically become Jesus' deeds which Matthew has reported. Second, the verses are colored by the saying (vss. 28-30) about the "easy yoke" which Matthew attaches to them. This is of great significance, since the "yoke" in Jewish Wisdom literature is never spoken of as the *teacher's;* it is always Wisdom's own. Thus once again Jesus is identified with Wisdom.

Now Jewish thought also identified Wisdom with Torah, and the rabbis could speak of the "yoke of the Torah." Thus when

Jesus invites his hearers to take his yoke upon them, he is inviting them to the Torah. Suggs concludes: "Jesus speaks as Sophia, and in such a saying as 11:28-30 that means *as* Torah as well" (106).

The close association Suggs finds between Jesus and the Torah is consonant with my own insistence upon the ultimately ethical character of Matthew's soteriology. Further, Suggs is lead to find a functional equivalent of the Pauline grace precisely in Matthew's doctrine of Law (108, 120). And in this respect also his conclusions parallel my own. On the other hand, Suggs's contention that for Matthew Jesus is Torah incarnate presents some difficulties for my argument. For if Jesus and Torah are identical, then it might be argued that Matthew is, after all, insisting upon an explicit and systematic union of christology and soteriology that renders ineffective his implicit appeals to human experience in general. And while it would be appropriate, from a Whiteheadian perspective, to subject this union of soteriology and christology to a critique, Sugg's position nevertheless means that we would have to reckon with Matthew's explicit intention to deny the point I am making in my emphasis upon the extra-confessional strains in his thought.

There is no question but that Suggs has discovered an intentional emphasis upon Matthew's part. But what, in fact, does he actually demonstrate in this regard? Apart from 11:19 all his evidence really shows is that, *as over against Q,* Matthew rejects the notion of Jesus as one of Wisdom's envoys and assigns to him sayings that were attributed to Wisdom in Q. Does this mean that Jesus is Wisdom incarnate, or does it mean simply that Matthew is reluctant to work with the somewhat suspect figure of Wisdom? Does Jesus speak *as* Wisdom, or has the category been largely supplanted? If Jesus is the Son of God—in the sense of being the divinely commissioned eschatological agent who stands in moral unity with the Father and whose function is to re-present the Torah at the climax of history—is it not quite natural that he stand in God's stead and issue both the word of grace and the word of demand? All this implies a great deal about Jesus' uniqueness and authority, about his climactic role in the history of salvation, but nothing about any sort of incarnation in his person.

The only passage that might be taken as indicating actual identity with Wisdom is 11:19. But even here another explanation seems more likely. Matthew's redaction shows that what is really at stake is Jesus' deeds, as Suggs rightly perceives. But if that is so, the most natural reading of the passage is in keeping with a de-emphasis upon the role of Wisdom as divine entity: the "wisdom" of Jesus' actions—understood, to be sure, as a wisdom given by God—is "justified by its results" (Johnson: 385). Although the personification of Wisdom is not obliterated, it is reduced to a metaphorical status. There is simply no need, on the basis of Sugg's evidence, to resort to a concept of incarnation in interpreting this gospel which seems so clearly to be oriented in another direction.

As Stendahl comments, the idea of sonship in 11:25-30 "has no clear implication of pre-existence or specific Christological speculation . . ." (784). Jesus' status as the revealer can be understood here simply in terms of his appearance at the climax of Israel's history as the one born Messiah and thereby given the authority of God to carry out the divine plan of salvation. While Jesus is indeed the one true revealer, designated by birth as Messiah, his special relation to God need connote no more than his unique authority and moral unity with the Father. Such, indeed, would seem to be the import of the temptation story (4:1-11) within the context of Matthew's prologue (see Thompson, Krentz).

With respect to Torah specifically, it is again unnecessary to speak of incarnation or identity on the basis of Suggs's evidence. That Jesus may speak of the "yoke" of the Torah as "my yoke" need mean only that he is the definitive interpreter of the Law by virtue of his eschatological office. If an actual identity were intended, would it be too much to expect that at some point Matthew might indicate it explicitly? Matthew's Jesus does not say, "I am the Law," but rather, "I came to fulfill the Law." As far as I can see, then, Suggs's treatment of 11:25-30 necessitates no revision of my earlier conclusions.

The one remaining element in the present passage which presents a serious problem for my case is found at 11:27b-c: "and no one knows the Son except the father, and no one knows the father except the Son and any one to whom the Son chooses to reveal him." The exclusivism of the statement is obvious. All knowledge of God is grounded in Jesus' relationship to God; God can be known only through relationship to Jesus—a relationship, moreover, which can only be granted by Jesus in seemingly deterministic fashion. If taken with full seriousness, this passage would tend to submerge Matthew's appeal to human experience in general under the weight of an explicitly exclusivist confession and a determinism of grace. What must now be established, however, is to what extent and in what way the exclusivism and determinism of the passage actually function in Matthew's thought.

Relevant to the question of determinism is the passage concerning Peter's confession: 16:13-20. The interesting point is that the reference to God's self-disclosure is set side by side—in the very same verse (17)—with a commendation of Peter for rightly perceiving Jesus' status. Matthew does not seem to interpret the statement that God has revealed this to Peter as obviating Peter's own freedom and responsibility. By analogy, then, we may assume that he does not intend for 11:25 to be interpreted in such a way as to deny human responsibility. The voluntaristic element in Matthew is, after all, attested as redactional, whereas 11:25ff. is taken from Q. And while Matthew must appropriate its content in *some* way, what it means to him is not necessarily the most apparent rendering. But, again, if there is no real paradox here, there is nevertheless tension: 11:27, if taken literally, says that those alone know God who are *chosen* by the son, implying that some unfortunates remain unchosen. If it is clear that Matthew does not mean this, he has nevertheless allowed himself to say it.

The exclusivism of the passage appears on the surface to be a much more serious problem. If I am correct in reading 11:25-30 in close conjunction with the problem of the Pharisees' rejection of Jesus, however, the exclusivist element here plays a very specific and limited role in the thought of the gospel. This passage, like much material in Matthew, functions both with reference to the

situation obtaining during Jesus' life and as exhortation to the
contemporary community. Verses 28ff. in particular would be
valuable as an appeal to the members of Matthew's church. On the
other hand, in light of what we know about the context of the
passage, the opening verses would seem to be of interest primarily
as a means of dealing with the historical problem of Jesus'
rejection. If this is so, then the exclusivism of the passage is
actually intended to bring Jesus' salvation-historical significance
to the fore. What is at issue is the Jews' failure to recognize the
Messiah who, according to God's plan, appeared in their midst.
The passage, on this view, states that in Jesus God's history of
salvation came to its culmination and that to miss what was taking
place in Jesus was to miss out on God's whole scheme of salvation,
to bypass God's eschatological representative to whom his
authority had been given. Such a failure could be interpreted only
as failure to know God. One could not reject Jesus and truly know
God; hence response to Jesus was the sole means of relating
oneself to what was happening *at that moment in history*.

It might be said, then, that the exclusivism of this passage
actually functions in a "kairological," rather than an ontological
sense. Matthew does not draw out the implication that no person
in the history of the world ever has known or ever will know God
apart from Jesus. Such an implication is implicitly contradicted
by his scheme of salvation-history. He probably does mean to say
that no one who rejected Jesus' earthly ministry knew God (see
12:25-37), and it is possible that he also means to say that anyone
who now explicitly rejects the gospel fails to know God. But that
there is absolutely no knowledge of God apart from Jesus or the
Church is not a point that Matthew actually makes in any way. In
terms of strict logic, of course, that is precisely what the passage
implies. Matthew expresses his kairological exclusivism in the
form of an ontological exclusivism. The question, though, is how
this latter element—along with the deterministic implications of
vss. 25, 27—is to be weighted in relation to the implications of
Matthew's appeal to human experience in general. My answer to
this question will appear as I bring the process perspective more
explicitly to bear upon the passage as a whole.

I begin, again, by noting the primary lures coming to expression in the passage. 1) The first segment of the pericope (vss. 25-26) directs the readers' attention to God as the source of revelation. But this general directive can be broken down into three component lures: a) a tacit "reminder" of the revelation already received by the readers—i.e., a re-presentation of the Christ-confession—seen in the fact that it is Jesus who offers the prayer; b) a direct lure to apprehend—in awe and reverence—the graciousness of God in freely *giving* this revelation; c) a negative lure toward rejection of the wisdom of the Pharisees, from whom the truth is "hidden." 2) The second segment (vs. 27) calls attention directly to Jesus as the bearer of revelation. Two component lures function: a) a positive lure toward the recognition of Jesus' supreme authority as God's decisive bearer of revelation; b) a negative corollary of the positive lure—an indication of the lostness that belongs to existence apart from Jesus' revelation. 3) The final segment (28-30) contains a similar set of corollaries: a) a positive lure toward a feeling of comfort, peace, "rest"—i.e., an apprehension of grace emanating specifically from Jesus' gracious command; b) an implicit negative complement—derivative from the redactional placing of the passage—toward a rejection of the "legalism" of the Pharisees.

Now it is clear from the context of the passage that the final set of lures has a functional primacy in Matthew's structure. The evangelist wants to contrast Jesus' "easy yoke" with the legalistic demands of the Pharisees. But the opening verses provide a background for understanding the grace given in that yoke: readers are drawn both to the Jesus of the Christian confession and to the God whom he represents. Moreover, it is quite clear that the lure toward reverence before God takes precedence; one apprehends Jesus precisely as the one who *thanks* God.

In a sense, though, the passage reaches its apex in the middle section. But one must be precise in describing the function of the lures here present. That function, it seems to me, is to *ground* the lure toward Jesus' own revelation precisely in the grace of God as addressed in the opening verses. The major point is to see in Jesus' word God's own authority. The corollary is a negative reaction to competing authority. But the negative lure clearly serves the positive; insofar as the negative is really functional as such, it is directed toward a denial not so much of all knowledge of God outside Jesus as of the Pharisaic claim to knowledge. So it is legitimate to ask to what extent the exclusivism entailed in a univocal reading of the passage functions in any meaningful sense and to what extent it is simply an emphatic accompaniment to its positive corollary.

If we remember that truth-judgments and logical precision are less important than other types of feelings, it would appear that tension between the primary function of the passage and its literal meaning presents no great cause for concern. The fact is that some truth-judgments in the passage have a functional relevance that others do not. A judgment regarding the yoke of Jesus as truly expressive of God's will—and therefore about Jesus as in fact representing God, and hence also about God himself—would seem necessary to the function of the pericope. A lure toward these judgments provides the cosmic context which grounds the entire thought-complex. But the same can hardly be said of the exclusivistic and deterministic corollaries. They serve primarily to underline the positive affirmations, for what is finally important is the call to Jesus as revelatory of God's actual will, not the affirmation that God "hides" himself from the Pharisees or that God makes himself unavailable apart from Jesus. The *functional* meaning of the exclusivistic element is that if Jesus represents the truth, rejection of him must mean rejection of the truth and that if Jesus and the Pharisees disagree, both cannot represent the truth. The *functional* meaning of the deterministic element is that the knowledge of God Jesus brings is in fact the knowledge that God graciously gives.

Now 11:25-30 does not contain an extra-confessional element as do 5:45b, 19:4ff., 8b. It is important, rather, because it exhibits Matthew's Torah-based soteriology as a soteriology of grace and because its seeming challenge to Matthew's universalistic lures turns out, under examination, to fade away. The tension between its literal exclusivism and its functional meaning is dissolved through a recognition of the way its various lures interrelate.

While it does not offer direct confirmation of Matthew's extra-confessional thrust, then, it does not call that thrust into question. And it is perhaps not too much to say that it even offers an indirect kind of confirmation. For it reveals how, in one case at least, a severely exclusivistic confessional lure is actually grounded in and serves a non-exclusivistic (although not explicitly universalistic) confessional lure with implications for the nature of reality in general. Hopefully, too, my analysis of the interaction of the various lures adds confirmation to the relevance of the Whiteheadian model, since it shows, again, how a non-univocal reading of proximate lures actually serves to emphasize the reference of the broader ones. That is not to say, of course, that the broader lures are themselves to be taken univocally, but only that the truth-judgments for which they call are to be taken more seriously than those to which the proximate lures apparently point.

My reading of the passage depends, to be sure, upon a demonstration that the exclusivist theme does not function meaningfully elsewhere in the gospel. If the inverse could be shown, we would have to reckon with Matthew's explicit intention to make an exclusivistic claim for its own sake. Thus my reading must remain tentative at present. And the same must be said in relation to the entire characterization of Matthew's soteriology presented in this chapter, since there are various relevant aspects of Matthew's thought not yet explored. But if it remains to be shown that this vision is not contradicted by the broader reaches of Matthew's christological thought, the more immediate question is whether the extra-confessional lure of which we have seen slight traces appears elsewhere in the gospel and constitutes a genuinely functional aspect of Matthew's soteriology.

In summary, the treatment of Matt 5:17-20 and 11:25-30 has hopefully demonstrated my two preliminary theses: Matthew's soteriology is based upon Torah, but this Torah functions precisely as grace. It has also uncovered, however, in the extra-confessional or universalistic lure, an undercurrent of thought wherein the entire covenantal dimension of the evangelist's witness is implicitly transcended. If this undercurrent can be further substantiated, it would seem possible to claim that my use of a process hermeneutic meets the test of "depth" by exposing a dimension of the text not immediately visible from other perspectives.

NOTES

/1/   See, e.g., V. Hasler, who perceives the centrality of 5:17-20 to the Sermon as a whole but misses the relationship between 5:20 and 6:1-18.

/2/   The fact that a close parallel to vs. 18 appears at Luke 16:17 might seem to indicate that Matthew took the verses from separate sources. But Schürmann shows that Matthew was familiar with a portion of Q which is preserved in Luke 16:14f., 16-18. So if a credible reason can be given for Luke having omitted vs. 19, the simplest solution is to attribute both verses to Q. And, in fact, such a reason is readily discernible. The larger Lukan context, 16:1-31, is unified not by the problem of the Torah but by the question of poverty and riches. Luke 16:17 serves well as a *theoretical* introduction to the saying on divorce, which would be helpful in dealing with the question of the indissolubility of marriage. But vs. 19, which is not theoretically oriented, would have no place in Luke's gentile community.

/3/   See Luke 16:14f., 16-18. Further, there is a subtle discrepancy between the notion of the Kingdom presented in vs. 20 as over against that in vs. 19. In 20, the offenders are excluded from the Kingdom altogether, while in 19 they are merely relegated to an inferior position.

/4/   See, however, Bultmann (1963: 138), who argues that vss. 18f. accrued to vs. 17, which he takes to be an authentic saying of Jesus, during the debates within the Palestinian communities concerning Jesus' attitude toward the Law. But the link between 18 and 19 is far stronger than that between 17 and 18. Given the cruciality of this passage, both structurally and thematically, it would seem highly likely that Matthew himself is responsible for introducing 17 into the context. An interesting suggestion is also made by Kilpatrick (26), who thinks vs. 17 may have been part of the M-source. In his reconstruction vs. 17 would have preceded 21f. which, in turn, would have been followed by 33-34a in part, 19f., 6:1-6, 16-18. This progression makes good sense, but Kilpatrick himself is somewhat unsure in assigning vs. 17 to it. Another possibility is that Matthew composed the verse himself precisely in order to reinterpret 18f. for use in the present context.

/5/   This would be consistent with Eduard Schwiezer's findings regarding Matthean usage of the term πληροῦν in reference to fulfillment of prophecy: "πληρόω is always to be understood as 'to bring to realization'; the object of the 'realization' is always the words of the prophets (in general or individually); this 'realization' always takes place in the life and death of Jesus" (482).

/6/   I must also oppose A. M. Honeymann, who argues as follows: "The clause ἕως ἂν πάντα γένηται. . . expresses in positive terms what is negatively expressed in the previous clause. The force of ἕως is inclusive and not temporal but modal,— '. . . to the extent, so that (on the contrary) all (of it) will be fulfilled'" (142). This passage affords an excellent example of the way in which a purely grammatical approach to such a question can be highly misleading. It is simply irrelevant to drag up possible Aramaic equivalents, as Honeymann does, when an exegetical examination of parallel expressions (Matt 24:34, Mark 13:30, Luke 21:32) shows rather clearly that the Greek expression has a temporal, rather than a modal, sense.

/7/   See also Ljungman: "'To do' means precisely that the Law 'comes to pass' and that the smallest part of the Law will not 'give way,' or 'be lost.' 'To do' in v. 19 corresponds with 'come to pass' in v. 18" (52). Thus γένεσθαι is read as an equivalent of ποιεῖν. W. D. Davies (1957) challenges this, arguing that this weight would better be born by the term πεπλήρωσαι. This is a serious challenge, but Schweizer has given convincing reason for interpreting ἕως ἂν πάντα γένηται in relation to the disciples' obedience. The question has been debated so widely that I feel it necessary to set out Schweizer's tightly-knit argument in some detail.

First, the phrase is drawn from the similar phrase at Mark 13:30, which clearly refers to the occurrence of what was prophesied. Second, at three points in Matthew we find a related formula (τοῦτο δὲ [ὅλον] γέγονεν—1:22, 21:4, 26:56) always in conjunction with a form of πληροῦν. In each case this latter term indicates that a prophecy is fulfilled in the life of Jesus. Since vs. 17 speaks not only of the "law," but of the "law and the prophets," it is clear that for Matthew "πληρῶσαι τὸν νόμον ἤ τοὺς προφήτας means what it means everywhere else: (salvation-historically) 'to bring to realization' precisely through the coming of Jesus" (481). So the peculiarly Matthean usage of γένεσθαι justifies its interpretation here as having to do with the fulfillment of the commands of the Torah, through performance. We might thus paraphrase vs. 18 in this way: "Until the eschaton, nothing will pass away from the Torah until authentic obedience to it takes place." But against the supposition that it is Jesus' own obedience that is envisioned here, Schweizer argues as follows. The phrase "law and prophets" occurs in two other places in Matthew—the Golden Rule at 7:12 and the double love-commandment at 22:40. In both instances Matthew has shaped the material to make the point that the "law and prophets" hang upon the love-commandment. Matthew's theological interest in the "law and prophets," then, has to do specifically with obedience to the Torah through adherence to the summary commands to love. Thus "as the bringer of this new commandment, which contains in itself the whole Law, Jesus appears in the following sections as the fulfiller of the Law and of the prophets" (482). Accordingly, "the Law and the prophets perpetuate themselves in relation to the Messiah's fulfillment-bringing deed in his community. Where that happens not a single commandment is abrogated—it is indeed fulfilled here" (483).

/8/   Ljungman is correct (67-75) in arguing that περισσεύειν in vs. 20 cannot be taken in a quantitative sense, as if the "higher righteousness" demanded were simply stricter attention to the "jot and tittle" of vs. 18. Such an attitude is condemned in 23:23f. The difference intended is clearly qualitative, involving obedience to God's own will as expressed in the command to love. Thus it involves setting God's will against some elements in the Law. But Ljungman's Paulinizing interpretation of this pericope is hardly the only alternative to a "legalistic" reading. As an indication of the hidden assumptions which color Ljungman's treatment, I quote the following: "Could it mean that Jesus came, after the manner of the prophets, to preach the whole content of the Law by summing it up in the commandments of compassion, righteousness, and faithfulness, or in the injunction to love God and the neighbor? Were this the case, it should have to be noted that such formulations were not foreign to the Judaism of Jesus' time. Judaism knew not only innumerable commandments and prohibitions, but also a unity in this multiplicity." Ljungman's assumption is that we must find a clear difference between Matthew's Jesus and Judaism. Granted that Matthew sees such a difference, we cannot simply assume that his view is historically correct.

/9/   It is significant that Matthew himself is responsible for the present form of vss. 21-48. Three of the antitheses imply actual changes in the Law (third, fifth, sixth), while the other three (first, second, fourth) involve only intensification or deepening of what is written (see Davies, 1957). And a comparison of 5:1-32 with its parallels (Matt 19:9, Mark 10:11-12, Luke 16:18) reveals that Matthew has constructed the antithetical element here. However, there is strong evidence of a pre-Matthean source behind the first, second, and fourth antitheses (Davies, 1957: 438). Thus it would seem that Matthew has taken an earlier triad and worked it into a longer series. The effect is the radicalization of the earlier form by inclusion of material implying a critique of the written code and the justification of this radicalization in vss. 17-20.

/10/   According to Daube, the introductory formula is based upon the phrase *shomecᵃ ʾanî* (I hear, I might understand), "which introduces an interpretation of Scripture which, though conceivable, yet must be rejected" (55). This consideration explains how the phrase "you have heard" could refer to commands not explicitly stated in the Torah: "The clauses 'and only he who kills shall be in danger of the judgment,' and 'thou shalt hate thine enemy,' do not occur in the Pentateuch at all. However, as soon as we proceed from the translation 'Ye have literally understood,' the additions cease to be troublesome. 'To understand' does not necessarily introduce a strict quotation; the quotation may be provided with a comment. The Rabbis remark on the fifth commandment: 'I hear, I might understand, Honour with words only.' Just so, Matthew writes: 'Ye have literally understood, Thou shalt not kill and only he who kills shall be in danger of the judgment'" (56). There is good reason, then, to see in Matthew's antitheses a revised form of a typically rabbinic mode of argument. If this evidence is accepted, Jesus' "fulfilling" commandments cannot be seen as a "new Law." They bring out the "old" Law's deepest intention.

/11/   It would be erroneous to argue that Moses' "concession" actually obviated responsibility to God's purest will, since Matthew's reconstruction of the dialogue gives the reference to creation a polemical tone. The point is that Moses made the concession because of the peoples' imperviousness; the implication is that they should have been able to bear the more rigorous command that God always intended.

/12/   Thus Stendahl's comment (789) to the effect that Gen 1:27 and 2:24 are "pre-fall" sayings and therefore weightier is not entirely to the point. The appeal is, to be sure, to the fact that the implied injunction is "more original," but the greater originality stems directly from the fact that these passages describe God's act of creation.

/13/   De Kruijf presents a detailed argument for understanding the passage in light of a Danielic context as the original background. He maintains not simply that the passage is grounded in the parallel logion at Dan 2:33, but that the thought-development of the context of Matt 11:25-30 corresponds to the thought-development of the opening chapters in Daniel. This claim is somewhat dubious, though, in light of the atomistic exegetical practices of the ancient world. Actually, the elaborate argument from the Danielic context is unnecessary to de Kruijf's major point. What he maintains about the passage in its Matthean setting is quite visible simply on the basis of that setting. Davies (1953), for instance, can say that "taken strictly in the light of its context the *tauta* [these things] in Matthew [11:25] refers to the woes on the cities of Chorazin and Bethsaida; what has been revealed is the eschatological significance of events of which judgment upon Chorazin and Bethsaida are a part" (137).

Part IV

The Undercurrent:
An Incipient Universalism

What I hope to show now is that Matthew's assumption of a soteriological principle transcending the Christian economy of salvation actually functions in the gospel. The evidence for this claim is to be found in two key pericopes—25:31-46 and 13:36-43, both of which unite the themes of eschatology and ecclesiology and thus constitute important links in Matthew's soteriological scheme. My contention is that if the subtle universalistic lure we have already noted in relation to Matthew's understanding of Torah appears in other lines of thought through which the evangelist works out the dynamics of his christology, then it may indeed be said to function in his conceptual scheme, whether or not he explicitly acknowledges it. To be sure, the results of this investigation will still have to be checked against Matthew's more directly christological statements, and that project will be pursued in chapter 9. But in light of the evidence that Matthew's understanding of Torah has led him to expose his universalistic assumptions, it is now relevant to ask whether the same is true of his eschatology and ecclesiology.

Chapter 6

The Explanation of the Parable of the Tares: Matt 13:36-43

36) Then he left the crowds and went into the house. And his disciples came to him, saying, "Explain to us the parable of the weeds of the field." 37) He answered, "He who sows the good seed is the Son of Man; 38) the field is the world, and the good seed means the sons of the kingdom; the weeds are the sons of the evil one, 39) and the enemy who sowed them is the devil; the harvest is the close of the age, and the reapers are angels. 40) Just as the weeds are gathered and burned with fire, so will it be at the close of the age. 41) The Son of man will send his angels, and they will gather out of his kingdom all causes of sin and evildoers, 42) and throw them into the furnace of fire; there men will weep and gnash their teeth. 43) Then the righteous will shine like the sun in the kingdom of their Father. He who has ears to hear, let him hear."

Matt 13:1-52 is a discourse made up essentially of parables of the Kingdom. Its main thrust is revealed in the opening and closing parables: that of the Sower (vss. 1-9) illustrates various responses (positive and negative) to the Kingdom, while that of the Drag-Net (vss. 47-50) refers to the final purgation in such a way as to constitute a warning to the Church. The ecclesiastical application is underscored by vss. 50-52, which conclude the discourse /1/. Jesus makes certain that the disciples have understood the lessons he has taught, thus anticipating the theme, woven into the narrative section 13:53-17:27, of the preparation of his followers for the time of the Church when he will no longer be with them /2/. The call to decision about the Kingdom also looks back to the preceding narrative, 11:2-12:50, which deals with Jesus' rejection by his people. Thus the evangelist's historical accounts of the rejection of Jesus and the founding of the Church are entwined with an exhortatory appeal to his own contemporary congregation: in the face of the coming judgment, Matthew's people, too, must make a decision about Jesus—whether to accept him, and gain the Kingdom, or reject him, and lose everything.

Rather clearly, both the Parable of the Tares (vss. 24-30) and the Explanation (vss. 36-43) are used to emphasize this very point /3/. They are above all warnings against false security. The point is that Church membership, confession of Christ per se, does not guarantee final entry into the Kingdom. The Church, too, must stand under God's eschatological scrutiny. Until that time, good and bad will exist side by side (29-30a); at the judgment, however, they will be separated (30b-d, 41; cf. also 49f.). The hortatory intent is evident in the admonition in vs. 43: "He who has ears to hear, let him hear."

That Matthew explicitly intends such a reading is supported by the fact that a similar pattern appears in the Matthean redaction of the Q Parable of the Wedding Feast (Matt 22:1-14 // Luke 14:16-24). Funk summarizes the peculiarly Matthean elements in three points:

> (1) the generalizing logion in 22:14; (2) the addition (or fusion) of the second parable, of the Guest Without a Wedding Garment (22:11-13); (3) the anticipation of the final separation by the phrase πονηρούς τε καὶ ἀγαθούς [both bad and good] in 22:10. (169)

The addition of the final separation 3) reveals one aspect of Matthew's concern. His eye is upon the evil-doers within the Church community, and he is explaining their presence. But the addition of the Parable of the Wedding Garment 2) and the logion in 22:14 1) together effect a shift from explanation to warning. If it is true that the Church contains both good and evil, this means that it will have to undergo a final purgation. The distinction between "the called" and "the chosen" in vs. 14 contains a summary of the entire point: many are called into the Church, but few will withstand the purgation and thus be "chosen" in the eschatological hour.

With respect to chapter 13, one may give essential approval to Bornkamm's comment that "the meaning of the coming judgment precisely for the Church is the aim of the whole construction" (19). But a closer look at vss. 36-43, the Explanation, shows that while Matthew's purpose is indeed to speak of the judgment which the Church will have to undergo, another theme is also allowed to function. It is important to note the relationship between the Church and the Kingdom in these verses. Some commentators have identified the Church with the Kingdom on the basis of 13:41, the assumption being that the Kingdom is a reality already existing, from which the angels will gather the elect. Bultmann's explanation, however, is surely correct: the elect will be gathered from the Kingdom "which will appear *then*" (1963:187, n. 3; see also Vögtle: 286f.). That the Kingdom is spoken of as the Son of Man's does not mean that it can be played off against the Kingdom of Heaven. For at 25:31-46 the Son of Man is again possessor of the Kingdom, but here it is clearly identified with the eschatological reign of God. The phrase, then, is not an ecclesiological expression (de Goedt: 44). And this judgment is congruent with the fact that the field, which is logically the pre-eschatological correspondent to "his kingdom," is expressly termed "the world." The world at large, as that which receives the seed, must be the scene of the sifting that is to take place.

Now this latter point is of profound significance. Vögtle has argued convincingly that, despite Matthew's ecclesiastical interest, and despite the explicit concern of the Parable of the Tares itself with the problem of "both good and bad," the Explanation centers simply upon the *fact* of the coming judgment (292)—in other words, upon a judgment of the world at large that also *includes* the Church. There is no narrowly ecclesiastical note in these verses—nothing, in other words, which undercuts the force of vs. 38: "the field is the world." And the criterion to be used at the judgment is distinctively Matthean: those condemned are "causes of sin and evildoers," and those received into the (purged) Kingdom are "the righteous." As we have seen, the contextual placing of the verses insures their ecclesiastical *application*. But the injunction issued to the Church is nonetheless based upon a general principle which cuts across Church and world. In Vögtle's words, although

> the decisive question is directed specifically at members of the
> Church—that is, at so-called good or evil Christians—it is
> nevertheless set forth in a basic and generally applicable
> fashion. It envisages the two mutually exclusive existential
> possibilities . . . which pertain to all men, irrespective of
> whether they are within or without the Church; as also the Son
> of Man assembles "all people"—Christians and non-
> Christians—before him at the final judgment (24:31ff.) to be
> separated and to receive their recompense, "every one
> according to his deeds" ([Matt] 16:27). (292)

Or as Strecker puts it,

> Church and world, accordingly, are delineated
> correspondingly. Both stand under the claim of the Kyrios,
> regarding the fulfillment of which they will be questioned at the
> final judgment; and both stand prior to that time as complex
> entities which contain both good and evil and assume man's
> accountability for his deeds. It is therefore the primacy of the
> ethical claim which assimilates Church and world to one
> another. It also prohibits an absolute distinction. The world is
> not as such negatively assessed; to the contrary, even in it there
> exists the possibility of salvation. (219)

These statements might seem too strong in light of the dual
image of the sowers. The sowing of the seed by the Son of Man is
surely a reference to the spreading of the Christian message into
the world (Vögtle: 289f.). Thus one might imagine that the
possibility of salvation, far from being inherent in the world, is
specifically a product of the Christian mission. In this case the
good seed would refer to the Christians and the bad seed to non-
Christians. But such a reading is impossible, since Matthew
knows quite well that there is bad seed within, as well as without,
the Church. The images of the good and bad seed refer—as vss.
41b, 43a show—to doers of good and doers of evil. Thus the
separation at the judgment seems finally to be carried out solely
on the basis of obedience, not on the basis of Church membership.
And if this reading stands, we have in 13:36-43 a clear example of

the functioning of a universalistic lure, for it will mean that when Matthew comes down to the crucial question of the ultimate criterion for salvation he reaches out to a standard that transcends his confessional witness.

There is, however, another way to read the passage. Jack D. Kingsbury accepts Vögtle's universalistic interpretation but adds an important qualification. His major point parallels Vögtle's:

> According to Matthean thought, those who will be accounted righteous at the Latter Day will quite simply be those who have done the will of God, i.e., those who have shown themselves obedient to the Law of God (as Jesus has handed it down) through this work of love exercised on behalf of the brother. But this reveals that the Matthean concept of righteousness is furthermore universal in outlook, for it cuts across cultic, ethnic, and institutional lines and establishes God himself as the norm for righteousness. (1969: 100)

More explicitly, he notes that the phrase τὰ σκάνδαλα (causes of sin) is used in an absolute sense, indicating that "Matthew's thoughts regarding the victims of those who give offense would seem to extend even beyond the confines of the Church" (1969: 103). Kingsbury qualifies this genuinely universalistic note, however, by interpreting it as relating solely to deeds of mercy done by non-Christians in relation to the Christian mission. He thus reads this passage in light of 23:13: "you shut the kingdom of heaven against men; for you neither enter yourselves, nor allow those who would to go in."

The major advantage of this reading is that it does allow the image of the Son of Man's sowing its natural reference—the mission of the Church. Jesus acts through his Church to raise up servants obedient to God's Law; Satan's action, however, creates disobedience—both by corrupting Church members and by hampering the progress of missionary activity.

But there is a problem here. Although the Son of Man's sowing would indeed seem to refer to the preaching of the Christian message, the image of Satan's sowing is more difficult to pin down. To the extent that it is limited to opposition to the Church, one must assume that the world per se does not stand condemned—i.e., that it is not already filled with bad seed. Thus one would have to admit that there is good seed in the world per se, unrelated to the Christian mission. Conversely, to the extent that the world is treated as condemned apart from the mission, the image of sowing bad seed becomes redundant. So if the logic of the Son of Man's sowing leads inexorably to a denial of the fully universalistic implication, the logic of Satan's sowing—because it assumes a "good" world as its background—leads inexorably to a recognition of that implication.

Kingsbury's way out of the dilemma, though, is apparently this: that for Matthew the world is in fact lost apart from the mission (cf. 1975: 149ff.), that this mission creates a new possibility of obedience, and that Satan's sowing is directed toward the stifling of this possibility in the midst of an otherwise corrupt world. And it must be admitted that such a scheme does solve the logical problem. Two assumptions, however, must be made for this solution to work. One is that Matthew's declaration that the gospel must "be preached throughout the world" before the end comes (24:14) means that literally every single human being in the entire world must be personally confronted with the gospel message before the final judgment comes. Only in this way can all evil in the world, with any credibility whatsoever, be attributed to explicit opposition to the Christian message. But 22:14 does not really say that every individual will hear the word; nor does 28:18, which speaks of "all *nations*" being made disciples. To get such a reading, we must not only go beyond the plain meaning of the words but also attribute to Matthew an astonishing naiveté not elsewhere apparent in his gospel. And it is quite unnecessary to do so, since two more likely readings suggest themselves.

One possibility is the view that Johannes Munck attributes to Paul—that the mission to "all nations" is meant in a representative sense (52ff.). Read in this way, the theme of the completion of the mission has to do with Matthew's salvation-history and not with a concern for an individual "chance" in the eschatological sweepstakes. Alternatively, Matthew could be saying, quite simply, that the mission will have gone out to the farthest corners of the earth—not necessarily even to every single nation, but in such a way as merely to symbolize the entire family of humanity—so that the salvation-history might run its course before the end. The reference to "all nations" could, in light of the "forceful and imaginative" (cf. Tannehill:11ff.) character of the passage, be understood as rhetoric.

So Kingsbury's qualification of Vögtle's universalism will not stand without stretching the meaning of 22:14 and 28:18. But it is still true that, apart from his qualification, the systematic character of the images of 13:36-43 breaks down. For on the one hand the "good seed" are identified with "good Christians"—products of the Church's mission who remain faithful—while on the other hand "good seed" are implicitly recognized in the world at large. So we must either accept the systematic view Kingsbury attributes to Matthew at the cost of a strained interpretation of 22:14 and 28:18 or be content with a high degree of tension in the language of the text.

A major factor in deciding this issue has to be an assessment of the second assumption behind Kingsbury's reasoning: that 13:36-43 is to be read in light of a particular understanding of 25:31-46, the Description of the Last Judgment, wherein the righteous and the unrighteous at the great separation are identified specifically and solely as non-Christians who have either helped or hindered the mission of the Church. There is actually nothing in 13:36-43 to indicate that evildoers are identified exclusively with those who oppose the mission or that all the good seed outside the Church are those who have aided it; such an implication has to be imported from 25:31-46. A conclusion about the meaning of the Explanation of the Parable of the Tares, then, will have to await a treatment of the latter passage.

Chapter 7

The Description of the Last Judgment: Matt 25:31-46

31) "When the Son of man comes in his glory, and all the angels with him, then he will sit on his glorious throne. 32) Before him will be gathered all the nations, and he will separate them one from another as a shepherd separates the sheep from the goats, 33) and he will place the sheep at his right hand, but the goats at his left. 34) Then the King will say to those at his right hand, 'Come, O blessed of my Father, inherit the kingdom prepared for you from the foundation of the world; 35) for I was hungry and you gave me food, I was thirsty and you gave me drink, I was a stranger and you welcomed me, 36) I was naked and you clothed me, I was sick and you visited me, I was in prison and you came to me.' 37) Then the righteous will answer him, 'Lord, when did we see thee hungry and feed thee, or thirsty and give thee drink? 38) And when did we see thee a stranger and welcome thee, or naked and clothe thee? 39) And when did we see thee sick or in prison and visit thee?' 40) And the King will answer them, 'Truly, I say to you, as you did it to one of the least of these my brethren, you did it to me.' 41) Then he will say to those at his left hand, 'Depart from me, you cursed, into the eternal fire prepared for the devil and his angels; 42) for I was hungry and you gave me no food, I was thirsty and you gave me no drink, 43) I was a stranger and you did not welcome me, naked and you did not clothe me, sick and in prison and you did not visit me.' 44) Then they also will answer, 'Lord, when did we see thee hungry or thirsty or a stranger or naked or sick or in prison, and did not minister to thee?' 45) Then he will answer them, "Truly, I say to you, as you did it not to one of the least of these, you did it not to me.' 46) And they went away into eternal punishment, but the righteous into eternal life."

The Description of the Last Judgment stands as the dramatic climax of Matthew's eschatological discourse and hence must be taken seriously as an expression of his own eschatology. This discourse is made up of three large blocks of material, each possessing internal thematic unity. Chapter 23 is a denunciation of the scribes and Pharisees. The section 24:1-36(35) is a detailed prophecy of the events of the end-time. The final piece, 24:37(36)-25:46, is a series of pericopes in which Jesus' followers are warned in the face of the coming judgment. The discourse as a whole is unified by the correlative themes of rejection of Jesus and eschatological judgment. Denial of Jesus—whether the explicit rejection by the Jewish leaders or the implicit rejection by Christians led astray—will be condemned at the final day. "Therefore," the evangelist concludes, Christians should "watch" (25:13) and "be ready" (24:44). Matthew thus picks up on the themes of judgment and the rejection of Jesus which appear in the preceding narrative (19:3-23:39). Here, as there, rejection is treated both as past history and as an issue in the living present.

The concluding pericope, 25:31-46, belongs to a genre ultimately dependent upon Dan 7:9ff., the classical instance of the judgment scene which achieved prominence in late apocalyptic material. The connection between ethical righteousness and survival in the hour of judgment is firmly embedded in the tradition of such scenes; what is distinctive is the theme of the "great surprise": neither the righteous nor the unrighteous are aware of the final reference or actual import of their deeds.

Whatever its background /4/, the passage has been accomodated to a christological framework. This is seen above all in the fact that Jesus as the Son of Man has become the ubiquitous referent of all good deeds done in the world. The surprise theme, however, points in another direction. Despite the fact that all ethical action is finally referred to Jesus, explicit confession of Jesus is not laid down as a requirement for salvation or as a prerequisite for right action. For this reason Strecker speaks of this passage in relation to 13:36-43 and 5:45 and sees, in all three instances, a salvation that transcends the boundaries of the Church:

> The Matthean apocalypse concludes with the picture of the judgment of the peoples; all the nations of the world are gathered together and judged—without respect to Church membership, but solely according to the standard of good works. . . . As with the Church, it is assumed that in the world of nations the good and the evil will remain together up until the ultimate separation at the final judgment. (218)

The universalistic interpretation of the passage has been widely disputed, however. Schlatter (726) and Schniewind (254), for example, readily admit that the salvation here depicted is available apart from Christian confession, but both interpret this fact by reference to what amounts to a Pauline framework: if Jesus here offers salvation apart from confession of his name, he does so on the basis of a forgiveness that has been won by his death. There is, however, nothing in the text to warrant such an importation of the theme of vicarious sacrifice. Unless it can be shown on other grounds that Matthew envisions a general forgiveness that creates a new possibility for human existence, that such a scheme actually functions in the gospel, then this interpretation cannot stand.

A more credible possibility is that suggested by Cope: the "needy" in the passage are Christian missionaries; the unrighteous are those non-Christians who have ignored their sufferings, while the righteous are those who have extended hospitality to them. Christians, then, are not here subjected to judgment at all. It is only outsiders who stand before the King.

There is actually a good bit of evidence that can be adduced in favor of this reading. The Son of Man refers to the needy as "my brethren" ($\tau\hat{\omega}\nu$ $\dot{\alpha}\delta\epsilon\lambda\phi\hat{\omega}\nu$ $\mu o\nu$), and "brother" ($\dot{\alpha}\delta\epsilon\lambda\phi\acute{o}s$) in Matthew generally means "fellow-religionist," except when referring to familial relationships (Jeremias: 109 and n. 82). Moreover, the qualifying phrase "one of the least of these" ($\dot{\epsilon}\nu\grave{\iota}$ $\tauo\acute{\upsilon}\tau\omega\nu$ $\tau\hat{\omega}\nu$ $\dot{\epsilon}\lambda\alpha\chi\acute{\iota}\sigma\tau\omega\nu$) appears, in the positive degree ($\dot{\epsilon}\nu\alpha$ $\tau\hat{\omega}\nu$ $\mu\iota\kappa\rho\hat{\omega}\nu$ $\tauo\acute{\upsilon}\tau\omega\nu$: one of these little ones) at 18:6, 10, 14, where it obviously refers specifically to believers. In vs. 6 it is even accompanied by the qualifier "who believe in me." It is however, 10:42 that "clinches the matter" for Cope: "And whoever gives one of these little ones ($\dot{\epsilon}\nu\alpha$ $\tau\hat{\omega}\nu$ $\mu\iota\kappa\rho\hat{\omega}\nu$ $\tauo\acute{\upsilon}\tau\omega\nu$) even a cup of cold water *because he is a disciple,* truly, I say to you, he shall not lose his reward." According to Cope, then, the judgment that takes place in 25:31-46 is a judgment of non-Christians only, and these are judged specifically in terms of their treatment of Jesus' representatives, his "little ones."

Two major arguments against this interpretation merit

consideration, however. First, the context of the passage shows that, whatever else Matthew may have in mind, he is thinking of the judgment upon the Church. For it is difficult to imagine that the series of warnings in the latter part of the discourse is concluded with a dramatic statement of promise/demand that does not in any way challenge the readers themselves. While chapter 23, the denunciation of the scribes and Pharisees, is directed to the crowds and the disciples together (23:1), chapters 24 and 25 are spoken to the disciples alone (24:1). Clearly, the conclusion at 25:31-46 would seem to be of a piece with the series of explicit (24:44, 25:13) and implicit (25:29-30) warnings that conclude the literary units preceding it. And the ecclesiastical reference is buttressed by a close parallel in rabbinic literature, cited by Jeremias (207; cf. Boers:68). In Midrash Tannaim 15:9 God addresses these words to Israel: "My children, when you gave food to the poor I counted it as though you had given it to me." As Boers comments, "Matthew probably understood the description in a sense similar to that of the Midrash passage, as an exhortation to fellow believers to aid their fellowmen when they are in need, but with Christ taking the place of God" (70).

It should be noted, also, that Cope's reading necessitates the assumption of *another* judgment—one specifically for the Church—either before or after the non-Christians are dispensed with. What seems unlikely is that Matthew would put such a dramatic scene to such limited use, particularly in view of the fact that it closes his major eschatological discourse.

The second problem with Cope's interpretation is that the supposed parallel with 10:42 turns out, under examination, to be false. Chapter 10 is an explicitly missionary discourse; the present discourse is simply eschatological in orientation, dealing with the general question of the endurance of all Christians to the end. And the phrase "because he is a disciple" at 10:42 serves only to distinguish that passage from the judgment pericope, where the "ignorance" of those ministering to the needy is the whole point of the passage: they do not *know* that the needy are "brothers."

The parallels to the phrase "one of the least of these my

brothers," however, cannot simply be overlooked. They constitute a strong argument in favor of viewing the needy as followers of Jesus, although by no means missionaries specifically. But what is the significance of this observation? Does it mean that those ministering to the needy are exclusively non-Christians, that the Church itself does not here stand under judgment at all? Let us note the way in which the term "little ones" is used in chapter 18. Who is it that Matthew's Jesus fears might lead his followers astray? Here again, Jesus is speaking specifically to the disciples (18:1); it is therefore the Church that receives a warning through them. The mention of those who "receive" the little ones (18:5) might conceivably be a somewhat out-of-context reference to non-Christians, but that cannot be the case in vs. 10—"See that you do not despise one of these little ones . . ."— or in vs. 14, which is followed by a bit of intra-ecclesiastical advice (vss. 12-20). If in chapter 18 it is Christians who are enjoined to care for members of their own community, there is no reason to deny that a similar theme is at work in 25:31-46. Who, after all, is most likely to visit Christians in prison? While Cope's interpretation has the advantage of attributing to Matthew a neat, systematic view of the passage, it misses the clear intention to enjoin Christians themselves to deeds of mercy. His interpretation fails, and with it goes Kingsbury's reading of 13:36-43.

But if we accept the ecclesiastical interpretation of the judgment scene, we are left with the problem that the passage clearly involves a universal context: that "all the nations" are gathered has to mean that non-Christians stand alongside Christians. So the curious result is that, logically speaking, non-Christians are included in a judgment based upon the question of whether one has ministered to his or her *fellow Christians*. And we cannot solve the problem by contending that the distinction between Christians and non-Christians has been obliterated (cf. Furnish:82f.) unless we are prepared to maintain that Matthew actually believes that the mission will reach every individual human being in the world before the end. Thus two possibilities remain: either the universalistic thrust of the passage is purely "accidental" and inconsequential or it has the effect of broadening the meaning of "little ones" actually to include, in a subsidiary way and by analogy, all human beings who stand in need. But there is no clear basis upon which to decide this question. So at this point it is pertinent to ask whether a process analysis can shed light upon the two passages in question, 13:36-43 and 25:31-46.

Chapter 8

A Process Analysis

We have been left with problematic results regarding both 25:31-46 and 13:36-43. The Description of the Last Judgment involves the implication that all the nations are judged by a standard that Matthew applies, in rather narrow language, to the internal relations of the Christian community. In the Explanation of the Parable of the Tares Matthew uses an image—"good seed"—that logically refers only to faithful Christians, but he in effect acknowledges the presence of other "good seed," beside that sown by the Church, at the final judgment.

One way of dealing with such results is to ignore the author's "aberrations" in favor of his general purpose. Matthew, after all, does not intentionally complicate his witness by injecting soteriological footnotes that stand in tension with his christology. Klostermann (205) and even Boers (68) can say that the universalistic note in 25:31-46 is *inadvertently* allowed to stand and imply that it is therefore insignificant. From a process perspective, however, an inadvertent theme may turn out to be of prime significance. Let us see, then, how an analysis of the various lures in these passages can illumine the role, if there is any, of the universalistic notes.

If my reading of Matt 25:31-46 is essentially correct, it should be apparent that the basic, over-all thrust of the passage can be defined as a lure 1) toward a feeling of compassion, or love, for the needy. Christians are, in an immediate sense, enjoined to care for the less fortunate within their community. In that this exhortation to deeds of love is sanctioned by an appeal to the eschatological judgment at which Jesus appears as Son of Man, however, the lure toward love is bracketed by an implicit recognition of its confessional context. There is thus an additional lure 2) toward recommitment of one's life to the Jesus who will appear as the Son of Man and judge. But Jesus serves as God's agent; so the call to recommitment to him actually opens into a lure 3) toward recommitment to the God whom he represents.

These three basic lures are inextricably bound up with one another. Service to the neighbor is considered service to Jesus; service to Jesus is considered service to God; service to God is (at least largely) defined as service to the neighbor. The picture is complicated, however, by a consideration of the theme of the "great surprise." As Boers says, because the acts of mercy are specifically recognized as not having been done in the name of Christ, the result is that "acts that are as such non-Christian, even though performed by Christians . . . are used to interpret the meaning of the confession of Christ" (72). What we have here, then, is evidence of the evangelist's tacit assumption of a genuinely universal standard of judgment which forms the basis of his injunction to the Church. Matthew actually "lets non-Christian acts interpret what the Christian confession really means," thus allowing the Christian message "to be confronted *and interpreted by worldly acts*" (Boers: 73; italics original). There is thus 4) a subtle universalistic lure that actually undergirds the lures toward confession of Jesus and love of Christians, and it parallels the universalistic lure seen elsewhere: one is implicitly asked to recognize the cosmic grounding of the love-standard simply on its own merits; it is, quite obviously, what God primordially requires of human beings.

But if this lure is recognized, there is no reason to deny, as Boers does, the functional import of the fact that it is indeed "all the nations" that are judged. "Inadvertent" though it may be, Matthew's placing of an ecclesiastically-oriented exhortation in the context of a universal judgment makes perfectly good sense when it is seen that the function of the tacit assumption of a universal standard is actually to ground the confessional lures. What Matthew says, in effect, is that Christians will be judged by the love-standard because that is precisely the standard which God will apply to *all human beings* at the final day. For love, after all, is the final expression of God's primordial will for human life. So Matthew's placing of the passage is evidence that the universalistic lure is part of the thinking process with which he is engaged.

Two important conclusions emerge from this discussion. First, the injunction to Christians to minister to fellow-Christians, by virtue of the fact that it is based upon the broader sanction of God's primordial will for human life, actually implies its own extension to include all persons who stand in need. Second, it appears that Jesus, the focal point of a particularistic confession, enforces a standard that is in fact universal, reaching beyond the very confessional tradition that proclaims him to be God's eschatological agent.

Now there is nothing problematic about the notion of a particularistic application of a universal standard. But the notion of an *exclusive representative* of a universal standard is self-contradictory. If the standard is in fact universal, and if the corollary assumption of the universal possibility of adherence is accepted, then the real possibility of *other* representatives cannot logically be denied. To the extent, then, that the particularistic lure toward confession of Jesus is understood as the proclamation of his exclusive status as God's representative, it must be seen as competing with the universalistic lure that stands in the background. Our question, then, is whether the particularistic lure toward confession of Jesus as God's eschatological agent must be understood as an assertion of his exclusive status as such.

The concept of "confession," it must be recognized, is highly ambiguous. It can refer to a pre-intellectual experience of ultimate commitment, or it can mean the discursive expression of that commitment. No linguistic formulation can be free of all discursive content; the question, though, is precisely which nuance, from among all the various connotations which the expression might suggest, is to be seen as determinative. The lure toward confession of Jesus as the Son of Man necessarily entails some kind of discursive explication of his role. It does, after all, entail an obvious claim to truth which has cosmic implications. But there are two fundamentally different ways of approaching such an explication, and they are correlative with the two primary ways of understanding the language in which the confession is made: the univocal, which takes the language as rigidly discursive, and the imagistic, which sees it as highly analogical or symbolic.

In either case, confession of Jesus means recognition of his objective role as a disclosure of God's eschatological standard. But a univocal explication entails exclusivity, while an imagistic does not. The reason is that a univocal reading gives place to certain negative corollaries entailed in a strict adherence to the logic of the confessional statement. If Jesus is the eschatological judge, then no other can stand in his place; if he is the one who appears at the apex of a salvation-history, as the revealer of God's primordial will, then no other can perform that function. His status—although not necessarily the salvation he brings—is thus utterly unique and therefore exclusive.

Univocally understood, then, Matthew's confession of Jesus proclaims him the exclusive representative of a standard Matthew tacitly recognizes as universal. And herein lies the root of the tension in the passage. What we have actually observed is the encroachment of a universalistic lure upon the strict logic of a confessional statement. An imagistic valuation of the confession, however, connotes only this as a minimum discursive affirmation demanding assent: that Jesus, in fact, represents God's eschatological standard. A claim of cosmic proportions is entailed, but an exclusivist assertion is not. Such a reading moves through the tension, without obliterating it, to identify a signification more basic than that which appears on the surface level.

Now Matthew himself interprets his christological confession univocally in the development of the mainstream of his thought. His salvation-history leaves no doubt that Jesus is the culmination of a series of events in which God has been uniquely active. This history, and it alone, is the divinely-initiated history of salvation. But the salvation that is the goal of this exclusive history is nevertheless defined, through Matthew's tacit lures toward recognition of God's primordial will, in a way that transcends the special events that achieve it. So the exclusivist corollaries of Matthew's confession stand in tension with his more basic assumptions. While the appearance of Jesus as eschatological judge and the reference of all deeds of mercy to him imply the exclusiveness of his role, then, the truth-judgment regarding this exclusivisty runs counter to the universalistic lure that grounds the confession itself by providing a broader sanction for Jesus' eschatological decisions.

This, in my estimation, is the crucial point that a Whiteheadian analysis exposes: *in that the universalistic note actually functions as the basis of the confessional lure, the meaning or point of the confessional element will have to be sought on the imagistic, rather than the univocal, level. In the present case, then, the christological witness forfeits its self-reference by serving as a lure toward a particular relationship with God—and hence toward certain truth-judgments about oneself and God—rather than as a straightforward truth-claim about Jesus' status.*

Our second passage, 13:36-43, is dominated by 1) a complex lure toward recognition of the fact of the coming judgment and the two possibilities that stand before the readers as Church members. The readers are lured toward recognition of the negative destiny of the evil ones as over against the positive destiny of the righteous and, obviously, encouraged to desire and therefore seek the latter. But the two existential possibilities are actually set within a confessional context, since it is of course the Son of Man's own angels that appear as the agents of the final separation. And the Son of Man, of course, is God's own representative. So we must speak also of less evident but functional lures toward recommitment to 2) Jesus and 3) God himself. In desiring eschatological salvation, the readers desire acceptance by Jesus as the Son of Man and ultimately acceptance into God's own Kingdom.

All these lures, however, are presented through the medium of an image of the judgment upon the world at large. And the judgment, as we have seen, is made solely on the basis of good deeds, without respect to Church membership. So Matthew does here precisely what he does at 25:31-46. He tacitly assumes a universalistic standard which serves to ground his ecclesiastical exhortation. In treating the question, "Will the Church be judged?" he implicitly raises the broader questions, "Who will be judged?" and, finally, "On what basis will judgment be carried out?" And he answers in this way: the Church will be judged, because all human beings will be judged; and all will be judged on the basis of their deeds. Once again, then, Matthew's confessional lures open into 4) a universalistic lure toward recognition of God's primordial will which provides the sanction for the confessional dimension.

If, then, the actual functioning of the broader lure is to be taken seriously, the christological lure will in this case also have to be understood imagistically rather than univocally. What is finally important is not assent to the discursive statement that the good seed are products of the Christian mission or that Jesus will appear as Son of Man and judge, but rather that the Jesus who is expected as Son of Man and, therefore, the Christian proclamation itself, do in fact represent God's universal standard of salvation.

It is possible, now, to draw a conclusion, contingent only upon an investigation of the mainstream of Matthew's thought. The gospel of Matthew does seem to contain an undercurrent of thinking that stands in marked tension with certain implications of the evangelist's christological witness. For at just those points where he works out the meaning of his witness to Jesus as the Christ—in his reflections upon Torah, the final judgment, the Church—Matthew allows a subtle lure toward a universal soteriological principle to place his christology in a broader framework of thought. Although he does not work out systematically the implications of his universalistic assumptions, these assumptions can nevertheless be said to function meaningfully in that they appear at just those points where the soteriological question is to the fore—i.e., where the crucial questions of who will be saved and of the criteria for salvation are answered. So the result is that the readers of Matthew's text are actually drawn toward a recognition of a principle that transcends the entire confessional dimension of Matthew's christology and which actually contradicts a univocal understanding of it. To the extent that readers follow up on the negative, or exclusivist corollaries of the christological lures, they find themselves in opposition to certain assumptions upon which that confession is based.

The import of this finding should be evident. If this valuation of Matthew's undercurrent is accepted, we have good reason to say that, at least in the case of Matthew, the point or meaning of christology, as Ogden and Braun contend, lies in its reference beyond itself to a quality of human existence before God—an anthropology, in the qualified sense used in this context—rather than in its claim regarding an exclusive act of God on behalf of human salvation. But there remain now the tasks of testing these results against some other aspects of Matthew's thought and of assessing the importance of the Matthean witness within the New Testament as a whole.

NOTES

/1/ Jeremias notes that the Parable of the Drag-Net is practically a replica of vss. 40-43 with a simple change of imagery. The shift, in fact, is not quite complete, since "it has been overlooked that ἐξελεύσονται [will come out] (vs. 49) is applicable to the reapers but not to the fishermen, and that ἡ κάμινος τοῦ πυρός [the furnace of fire] may describe the fate of weeds and straw, but hardly that of fishes." This close relationship between the two pericopes would seem to indicate that Matthew himself composed the latter, since it is hardly more than a collection of recurrent Matthean phrases to enforce a point. And that point is unmistakable. Matthew places it in its present context "as an allegorical description of the Last Judgment, a warning against false security" (85).

/2/ I concur with Krentz and Kingsbury (1975: 1-39) in their rejection of Bacon's analysis of Matthew's structure, in which each narrative unites with a discourse to form a "book," in favor of a recognition of major division at 4:17 and 16:21. I believe that both the discourse and the narrative sections can be shown to possess internal unity, however, even though it is sometimes loose. On the narrative at 13:53-17:27, for example, see ahead, ch. 9.

/3/   Cf., however, Kingsbury (1969:18), who thinks the parable itself deals with the relationship between Israel and the Church. I must reject this view, since it makes the interpretation in vss. 36-43 mean something different from the parable it supposedly interprets. Even though Jesus speaks to the crowds before vs. 36 and to the disciples afterward, the point of having an interpretation is to show the meaning of the original specifically for the Church. If the original is spoken to the crowds, this does not indicate that it must have a different meaning since the crowds, as vss. 10ff. show, do not understand anyway. And to the extent that Matthew's Jesus teaches the crowds, I should think, he teaches them as potential followers.

/4/   See Boers (63-70) for a discussion of the question of the background of the passage.

Part V

The Mainstream:
A Fragmentary Christology

Chapter 9

Jack D. Kingsbury has argued recently that Matthew's christological witness—rather than, e.g., his ecclesiology—is the central element in his gospel (1975). While his thesis might seem at first blush to stand in complete opposition to the view of Matthew presented in this study, this is not necessarily the case. The question I have raised is not whether Matthew intends to present a christology, or even whether that christology is, on the level of a descriptive exegesis, the controlling element in Matthew's scheme of thought. It is how a process analysis, designed to uncover not only Matthew's immediate intentions but also his most fundamental presuppositions, can shed light upon the relationship between that christology and the soteriology that accompanies it. And what I have hopefully demonstrated in the preceding chapters is that such an analysis reveals the importance of a strain of thought that in some sense overextends the christology that is admittedly central to Matthew's own intended scheme. The question that I will pursue in the present chapter is whether this universalistic undercurrent might not be rendered forceless by elements in Matthew not yet treated.

The essence of my argument has been that because the undercurrent appears at crucial junctures in the gospel, points at which Matthew works out the actual dynamics of his christology in soteriological terms, it is—even though it is not as such explicitly formulated—a genuinely functional element in the thought pattern of the gospel. An appreciation of the force of the undercurrent, however, depends upon a particular understanding of the mainstream. Thus, for example, if it could be shown that Matthew genuinely appropriates a notion of vicarious atonement and accepts Jesus' death as effecting a cosmic shift in the status of humanity before God, then my emphasis upon Matthew's voluntaristic approach to Torah-salvation would have to be qualified in some way. And any such qualification would of course affect the way in which the universalistic undercurrent is valued. Even more damaging to my argument would be evidence that Matthew actually intends explicitly to limit salvation to those who confess Christ, that he actually embraces an incipient doctrine of *extra ecclesiam nulla salus*. For this would constitute an explicit denial of the undercurrent I claim to have exposed.

I have no interest, then, in disputing Kingsbury's claims regarding the centrality of Matthew's christology to his total witness. But in that Kingsbury also makes parallel claims regarding related motifs such as atonement, it will be important to take his views into account as I seek to characterize Matthew's christology more precisely.

It is all but universally recognized that Matthew couches his christological witness in terms of a scheme of salvation-history. This scheme is particularly evident in two bodies of material—the introduction (1:1-4:16) and the core section (21:33-22:10) of the "parables against Israel" at 21:28-22:14 (see Kingsbury, 1975:7-17 and Krentz).

The introduction deals with Jesus' origins, both in the sense of the historical circumstances of his appearance and in the sense of his credentials as God's eschatological representative in whom scripture is fulfilled. Jesus is attested as Son of David, Son of Abraham, and Son of God. The genealogy plays a primary role at this point, emphasizing God's use of historical sequence in his project of salvation. There are three sets of fourteen generations, the divisions of which correspond to those in the Chronicler's scheme. Jesus' coming thus signals the seventh generation in a series of sets of seven and so initiates the Jubilee of Jubilees. At the end of the gospel Matthew is therefore able to present Jesus' mission charge in terms of Abraham's blessing (Gen 18:18), and the genealogy itself anticipates the influx of the gentiles by the inclusion of foreign women (Milton:175-81). Important also are the seven formula-quotations which attest the details of Jesus' infancy and pre-ministry as fulfillment of the scriptural witness: 1:22f.; 2:5f., 15b-c, 17, 23; 3:3, 4:14. The action of the Holy Spirit in the birth story is thus commensurate with the atmosphere of divine direction in the entire section and in the gospel as a whole.

Alongside the theme of the continuity of Jesus' advent with God's former activity there appears also an emphasis upon discontinuity with the past. Jesus comes as a sign of God's judgmental action (3:11f.) as well as of his saving activity. Already in the introduction, then, we have an indication of one of the most important aspects of Matthew's thought: his belief in God's freedom over against his agents, which allows him to apply the same standard of judgment against the Church that John the Baptist applies against Israel. The evangelist thus lays the groundwork for the presentation of Jesus as the Messiah rejected by Israel and now proclaimed to all the world. And he establishes a principle which undergirds his teachings and admonitions: God judges those among his servants who disobey him.

The final periocpe of the introduction, 4:12-16, signals the beginning of Jesus' ministry and the inception of a new epoch in salvation-history. The formula-quotation at 4:14 attests not simply the historical detail of Jesus' dwelling in Galilee as fulfillment of prophecy but also the significance of the whole turn of events which precedes that moment. The introduction ends upon a poetic note, taking up again the theme of salvation which appeared in 1:21b: this moment is the dawn of salvation.

Jesus' role in the scheme thus delineated is obviously a central one. As Kingsbury summarizes,

> Jesus, in the line of David (1:21), is the Son of God (2:15; 3:17), that is to say, he has his origin in God (1:20) and is the one chosen to shepherd the eschatological people of God (2:6) for, empowered by God for messianic ministry (3:16-17), he proves himself in confrontation with Satan to be perfectly obedient to the will of God (4:3-4, 5-7, 8-10) and, as such a one, he saves his (God's) people from their sins (1:21). (1975:52)

The "parables against Israel," taken collectively, have the effect of actually outlining the entire course of the history of salvation. The stage is set by the Parable of the Two Sons (21:28-32), which contrasts the unfaithful Jewish leaders to those among the tax collectors and harlots who are believers. The Parable of the Guest Without a Wedding Garment (22:11-14) concludes the series by using Israel's experience as a warning to the Church. In the two parables in between, however, Matthew reveals his attitude toward Israel and in so doing gives his understanding of God's dealings with his original people.

The Parable of the Wicked Tenants (21:33-41) is, in typical Matthean fashion, treated as an allegory. It alludes to the establishment of Israel as God's people (21:33), the sending and rejection of the prophets (21:34f.), the ministry and death of Jesus the Son of God (21:37-39), and, finally, God's turn from Israel to the gentiles (21:41). Jesus' comment which follows in vss. 42f. reemphasizes the latter point: because Israel rejects the "cornerstone," the Kingdom is taken away and given to a fruit-bearing "nation," the Church. The Parable of the Wedding Feast (22:1-10), again treated allegorically, adds an explicit reference to the destruction of Jerusalem (22:7) as punishment for Israel's failures and reiterates God's turn to the gentiles (22:8-10).

Clearly, Matthew intends to present Jesus as the Messiah-Son of God who stands at the apex of a continuing history of salvation and thereby effects salvation for humanity. The crucial question for the present study, however, is precisely how he does so. Kingsbury is convinced that a doctrine of atonement is at work. It is such a motif, he thinks, that informs the theme of Jesus' obedience to God employed in the temptation story and passion narrative:

> Since in Matthew's eyes the cross is the place where Jesus does shed his blood (cf. 27:22-26), it is here, through atonement, that he effects the forgiveness of sins. To Matthew, however, only one who relies upon God and renders to him perfect obedience can atone for sins, and this person, in turn, can be none other than Jesus Son of God, ideal Israelite (cf. Exod 4:22-23). (1975:76)

As evidence of the functioning of the atonement doctrine, Kingsbury points to three passages: 1:21, 20:28, 26:28. Each of these bears close scrutiny.

Hahn's comment on 1:21 is highly instructive. It has, he argues, nothing to do with an atoning death:

> Rather we must go back to the story of Zacchaeus, Luke 19:1ff. . . . There σωτηρία [salvation] is understood in the sense of the pardon of the sinner, and this Jesus grants by receiving the repudiated into his fellowship. (275)

One cannot, of course, prove that Matthew does not read an atonement theory into the traditional material. So perhaps all that can be said is that as it stands 1:21 is completely ambiguous of interpretation. One cannot prove the effectiveness of an atonement theology by merely pointing out that it is said here that Jesus "will save his people from their sins," for that phrase *can* be taken in the traditional Jewish sense that Hahn indicates. It must be shown on other grounds that Matthew intends to move beyond this sense to include the notion of the atoning quality of Jesus' death.

The atonement passages, 20:28 and 26:28, might in fact be interpreted as the evidence necessary to make just such a case. But these passages, it should be noted in beginning, are Markan material imbedded in immediate contexts that are also Markan. Thus while we must assume that Matthew appropriates their content in some sense, we cannot be certain that he interprets them in the most immediately apparent way. We must try, then, to discover Matthew's interest in the passages through an analysis of his editorial activity.

A reading of 20:28 is heavily dependent upon an understanding of its contextual placing, for the thought development of 19:16-20:28 is highly significant. The question about eternal life (19:16-22), with its concluding remark on riches, is followed, in dependence upon the Markan order, by sayings on riches and the Kingdom which conclude with a "first and last" logion (19:30). Between this point and the passion prediction at 20:17-18, Matthew adds the Parable of the Workers in the Vineyard, which is special-Matthean material and to which has been appended another "first and last" saying (20:16). Then, following the prediction, in agreement with Mark, comes the question of the mother of the sons of Zebedee (20:20-28) with Jesus' concluding remarks on serving and being served. Matthew's reconstruction of the context, then, creates a pointedly didactic unit built upon the theme of humility versus self-seeking. And his only change in 20:28 (// Mark 10:45)—the shift from κὰι γὰρ (for) to ὥσπερ (even as)—serves only to reemphasize the didactic point by playing up the theme of correspondence between Jesus and his disciples. Just as Jesus comes as the servant rather than the one served, so must those who follow him be willing to serve one another.

Thus the only interest Matthew betrays in his editing and placing of the passage is his persistent ethical concern, and Stendahl rightly comments that the didactic setting of 20:28 should warn us not to push too hard here for theological significance (790). In light of the role of Torah in Matthew's soteriology, though, it is perhaps best to put it this way: the only theological emphasis in the passage of which we have editorial evidence is precisely an ethical one. These considerations do not, of course, prove that Matthew sees no other theological meaning in the passage. But they should warn us not to assume lightly that he does.

If 20:28 cannot substantiate the atonement theme, what then of 26:28? This latter passage occurs within the context of Jesus' "words of institution" at the last supper (26:26-29), a complex which exhibits three significant changes over against Mark 14:22-25. First, the Matthean version adds the phrase "for the forgiveness of sins" to the end of the pericope. Second, the injunction to "eat" has been appended to the bread-saying. Finally, the phrase "and they all drank of it" in the Markan cup-saying (Mark 14:23) becomes "drink of it, all of you" in Matt 26:27. All these changes, Strecker observes, are in all probability due to liturgical tradition (222; see also Kilpatrick: 126). There is hardly another explanation for the shift to the imperative πίετε (drink) or the addition of the imperative φάγετε (eat) to Mark's λάβετε (take). And the addition of the word of forgiveness is easily attributed to the same motive.

There is, moreover, an important point of contact for our passage at 9:8 which strengthens this judgment. In editing the Markan story of the healing of the paralytic, Matthew seizes upon the word "authority" in Mark 2:10 (// Matt 9:6) and constructs a new ending in which the crowds marvel at the authority given "men." Strecker argues that this constitutes a reference to the community's power to forgive sins, since it is the authority to forgive that is at stake in the story. Thus, by analogy, at 26:28 the phrase "for the forgiveness of sins" is a reference to that forgiveness which the community dispenses through the cultic meal (221f.). The community exercises the authority given it by Jesus (10:1, 28:18) precisely by dispensing that forgiveness which Jesus himself issued while on earth.

If this emphasis upon the community's power of forgiveness is what is primarily intended by the phrase "for the forgiveness of sins," then one must be all the more careful about pressing these words for a statement of the atoning power of Jesus' death. While Matthew might formally acknowledge some kind of connection between Jesus' death and the forgiveness dispensed, it cannot simply be assumed that this connection is genuinely significant for Matthew's thought in the sense of actually affecting his soteriological scheme. Strecker is quite correct in saying that the atonement is certainly not the center of interest at this point, since the meal seems to be for Matthew more an act of obedience to Jesus' command than a theologically pregnant act. The liturgical imperatives added to the account of the meal suggest that it is to be understood

> on a level with the other instructions of the earthly Jesus for the life of the community and is therefore self-evidently a part of the eschatological δικαιοσύνη [righteousness]. The observation of it is therefore an act of obedience which does not raise questions beyond the demand of the Kyrios. . . . (222)

The burden of proof, then, is upon any interpreter who wishes to see a functioning doctrine of vicarious atonement in 26:28.

The real reason, I suspect, that Kingsbury is able to put so much weight upon the passages in question is that he treats the passion narrative itself as evidence of Matthew's interest in atonement (74-76). As Strecker again comments, however, the "mere fact" that Matthew uses the account of the passion "does not in itself justify the assertion of its atoning significance" (181). The question is not whether Matthew has adopted the atonement motif. There is, after all, no way of denying its formal presence in 20:28 and 26:28. What demands attestation, though, is that he actually appropriates its meaning, that he lets it inform his own understanding of the dynamics of salvation. One must ask whether he does not actually nullify the effect of that motif by his consistently ethical understanding of the righteousness that leads to salvation.

Another passage that has frequently been cited as evidence of Matthew's interest in atonement is 3:15, but I have already noted (see above, pp. 65ff.) that this interpretation is ill-founded. The real significance of Matt 3:15 is to be found only when it is read in light of Matthew's understanding of righteousness as obedience. Jesus undergoes baptism, quite simply, because it is in accordance with God's will; it is the obedience that God requires, just as at 28:19 Jesus institutionalizes the act by commanding its perpetuation in the community. So 3:15 actually lends support to Strecker's interpretation of the last supper as an act of eschatological righteousness performed for no other reason than that Jesus commanded it.

I must object, finally, to Kingsbury's use of the theme of Jesus own obedience to the Torah in relation to the atoning quality of his death (1975:51, 76). There is no question but that Matthew does emphasize Jesus' obedience. Such, indeed, is the point of the temptation narrative (4:1-11). Further, at 11:29 Jesus is described as "gentle and lowly in heart," and at 9:13 and 12:7 he interprets his own deeds as exemplifying the principle that mercy is the central criterion of Torah-interpretation. But the most obvious valuation of this motif connects it with the correspondence between Jesus and his disciples rather than with the theme of the sacrifice of the unblemished. As Bornkamm argues, Matthew links Jesus' role as teacher to his status as Christ, Son of God, etc., precisely by having him manifest this status by his own obedience to the Torah he proclaims (36f.). His obedience is thus an attestation of his authority and, as such, something which is to be delivered over to the Church for his followers' appropriation. Just as he fulfills what God demands of him by submitting to baptism, by overcoming temptation, and by carrying out his entire messianic commission, so the disciples are called to follow him precisely by obeying the demands of God made manifest in his teachings.

Now if an atonement theology does not function in the gospel, neither does the notion of a cosmic drama that effects a basic shift in the relationship between God and humanity. A negative judgment must be passed upon the significance Kingsbury attributes to the figure of Satan (149-57). It is unimpressive to point to passages such as the "strong man" saying (Matt 12:29 // Mark 3:27), which Matthew adopts from tradition, as evidence of an effective dualism in the gospel. Undoubtedly Matthew does see Jesus as defeating the power of Satan, and this means that he must reckon with Satan as having some kind of hold on the world. But his consistent voluntarism shows that he does not interpret this to mean that human beings are imprisoned by the power of sin or that obedience to God's will is impossible apart from some kind of cosmic upheaval. What is missing, once again, is any sort of evidence that Matthew takes this traditional motif with such seriousness that he actually allows it to shape his soteriological scheme.

A final problem remains. I argued earlier (see above, pp. 95f.) that the exclusivism in Matt 11:25-30 is "kairological," rather than ontological, claiming that Matthew does not in that passage give explicit endorsement to the notion that no knowledge of God was available prior to or apart from the revelation Jesus brought. I left open, however, the question whether Matthew might not present an ecclesiastical exclusivism, limiting all salvation *after* Jesus' time to the community within which he is proclaimed as Lord. And there is one passage that might be read in such a way as to support such a notion: Matt 16:16-20—Peter's confession and Jesus' saying on the "keys of the kingdom" /1/. For here Jesus says that Peter (as a representative of the Church; cf. 18:18) is to receive the keys and that whatever he "binds" on earth "shall be bound in heaven," and whatever he "looses" on earth "shall be loosed in heaven."

The traditional reading of this passage, however, in which it is seen as proclaiming the Church as the sole avenue to the Kingdom, does violence to the evangelist's intention as evidenced by his redactional activity. Peter's confession stands at the midpoint in a narrative section that embraces 13:53-17:27. The preceding half is somewhat loosely knit but is clearly dominated by the themes of the rising opposition to Jesus and his preparation of his disciples for the time when he will no longer be with them. The death of the Baptist (14:1-12), the opposition of the elders (15:1-20), and the pericope regarding signs (16:1-4) may be seen as directly related to the former theme; the feedings (14:13-21, 15:32-39) may be seen as fostering the latter. The story of the Canaanite woman (15:21-28) and the accounts of the healings (14:34-36, 15:29-31) may be understood as prefigurations of the salvation of the gentiles, so that while these segments of material do not constitute explicit preparation of the disciples they do lay the groundwork for the situation in which the post-resurrection Church will exist. Then, following the confession pericope, comes the first passion prediction (16:21-23), which Matthew has altered (cf. Mark 8:32-33) so as to constitute a crucial turning point in the gospel. It signals the beginning of the third (and final) major division of the gospel, in which Jesus' death and resurrection is the focus of attention (Kingsbury, 1975:7-25; also Krentz). Jesus' teaching, in this entire section, is dominated by explicit instructions to his disciples. Thus at 16:24 (// Mark 8:34) Matthew alters the Markan text by having Jesus speak only to his disciples of his coming death. And he introduces, at the close of the immediate narrative, the temple tax pericope (17:24-47) which, through its proclamation that "the sons are free," distinguishes the Church from the old Israel.

So the first thing that must be said with respect to Jesus' response to Peter's confession is that its context reveals its narrowly ecclesiastical import. Jesus here founds the Church precisely so that he may now begin to prepare the disciples for the post-resurrection situation. And an examination of 18:18, a parallel to the latter half of 16:19 in which the authority to "bind" and "loose" is given to the Church collectively, shows that these terms—whatever their precise meaning /2/—are to be understood as processes by which the Church carries out its own internal discipline. Thus when in the first half of 16:19 Jesus gives Peter the "keys of the kingdom" he evidently gives him some kind of guardianship over the means by which the individual Christian believers relate to the Kingdom. So the passage in question does not deal at all with the matter of the exclusivity of salvation offered by the Church, but rather with the problem of who among the believers will be saved.

The impression of explicit exclusivity derives from the image of the keys. Traditional interpreters have assumed that if Peter holds the keys in the name of the Church, then of course none can enter who are not numbered among the flock. But if Matthew's purpose is to deal with the question of which Christians will enter the Kingdom, then nothing whatsoever—positively or negatively— is implied with respect to non-Christians. If one wishes to push the logic of the image, it will move just as easily in another direction: the existence of one set of keys says nothing about how many duplicates might be available! To argue this way, of course, is to miss the point of the passage. But so, by the same token, is the attempt to see here a doctrine of *extra ecclesiam nulla salus*. As far as I can see there is no reason to believe that Matthew explicitly intends to limit all future salvation to that effected through the Christian economy.

It would appear impossible, then, to show that Matthew has in any way made an explicit denial of the incipient universalism constituted by his anthropological undercurrent. He presents no ecclesiastical exclusivism and does not allow an atonement theology to function meaningfully in his soteriological scheme. Moreover, by his persistent voluntarism he in effect denies that a cosmic shift is necessary to grant human beings the freedom necessary for authentic obedience to God.

So when we ask the question of the nature of Jesus' saving act, or of the shape of Matthew's mainstream of thought, we need not go beyond the scheme of salvation-history to which we have been continually driven. Because Jesus saves precisely by standing within that scheme and bringing God's plan to fruition, it may be said that in a sense *Matthew's christology is a function of salvation-history and not vice-versa.*

Jesus' definitive interpretation of the Torah, however, is not the simple creation of a new possibility of obedience, but rather presents a new occasion for that righteousness which was always required of humanity. Jesus' presentation of the higher righteousness is nothing other than the actualization of that possibility always present to Israel in the Torah. *So the Matthean salvation-history, together with the christological witness that stands at its heart, is in turn a function of Torah, and not vice-versa.*

The Torah that functions soteriologically is, of course, Israel's Torah as definitively stated by Jesus. But when Matthew makes Jesus' statement of God's will the implicit criterion for all humanity, applied subsequently to the Church, then the entire system of salvation-history is in effect transcended. So while it is true that on the level of the author's explicit intention Jesus saves through Torah within a scheme of salvation-history, in terms of the perspective on his total thought processes provided by a Whiteheadian analysis we must say that he saves simply by illuminating God's ever-present saving word of demand and grace. Thus *Torah itself, as a component in a covenantal theology, becomes a function of a broader standard and possibility available to humanity per se—which is to say, humanity before God.*

One might say, alternatively, that Matthew's undercurrent broadens the meaning of the term "covenant." In any case, the result of attending to the fundamental presuppositions revealed in Matthew's witness is this: the christological proclamation, which constitutes the mainstream of his thought, turns out to be an incomplete or fragmentary witness. For Matthew's soteriology, which is of course formally based upon his christological claims, actually overextends his christology in that the functioning criterion for salvation is broader than the Christian economy of salvation the evangelist intends to present. The christological witness is fragmentary because it is not really self-intelligible but depends upon a subtle undercurrent that actually grounds, interprets, and sanctions it. In terms of an exegetical description, of course, the undercurrent remains just that—an undercurrent—for it is merely presupposed and never stated and is evident only in light of a method designed to expose it. But this study has hopefully shown that it is present and does function meaningfully.

NOTES

/1/   Windisch, for example, sees here the doctrine of *extra ecclesiam nulla salus* (1928:165).

/2/   Allen argues that "bind" and "loose" translate technical rabbinic terms for "permit" and "forbid." On this basis he contends that the passage has to do with Peter's authority to pronounce on matters of morality and discipline, deciding which actions are "legal." The keys, then, would have to be understood in light of this legislative function: "St. Peter was to hold the keys, *i.e.*, he was to be supreme administrator; he was to bind and loose, *i.e.*, he was to be supreme legislator" (248-50). The thought development at 18:15-18, however, suggests that Matthew extends the terms to include the power of "excommunication"—which is, however, something different from absolute power over entrance into the Kingdom.

Part VI

Christology Beyond Dogma:
The "Catalytic" Christ

The question to which this final section will be devoted is this: What is the *significance* of the fact that a process analysis reveals a universalistic thrust in Matthew's christology? Matthew, after all, presents but one among many New Testament christologies—and one, moreover, that many interpreters might deem pale beside those of Paul and John and beside Jesus' own proclamation of the Kingdom. It is possible, in other words, to argue that Matthew's undercurrent places him outside the mainstream of New Testament thought as a whole. Thus in order to deal with the larger question of the meaning or point of *New Testament* christology on the basis of this paradigmatic study of Matthew, the place of this gospel within the whole must be determined. In chapters 10 and 11, accordingly, I will make a brief examination of several christological statements from the perspective assumed throughout the study and seek to show how a process analysis might be applied to the problem of assessing New Testament christology as a total phenomenon. Then, before a final summation, I will return to the question of a process methodology for some final observations.

Chapter 10

Outline for a Critique of New Testament Christology

Bultmann, in his *Theology of the New Testament,* sets Paul and John against those writings, within and without the canon, that involve no notion of a general release from the power of sin effected through Jesus Christ (1951-, Vol. 2:161ff., 203ff.). In Paul and John, he finds that the imperative is truly based upon the indicative. Braun expresses the same point by saying that in Paul and John there is a genuine union of christology and soteriology. In certain later writings, however, the human situation in Christ is not fundamentally different from the human situation as conceived in Judaism. In that Christ's death effects only forgiveness of past sin and not a general destruction of the power of sin, human beings are once more placed before a legal demand by obedience to which they are asked to achieve ethical righteousness as a condition of salvation.

Now there is much justice in Bultmann's description both of the Pauline-Johannine paradoxical union of christology and soteriology and of the loss of this paradox in later writings. But if my judgments regarding Matthew are sound, we have here a rather clear example of a way of explicating Jesus' salvific significance which unites the indicative with the imperative without reference to a release from the power of sin in the Pauline-Johannine sense. In this case Bultmann's tendency to consign all material not embodying a paradoxical view of Jesus' significance to the status of legalism appears unjustified. For if we do not have a prior view of the world as so literally and completely under the power of sin as to undercut the real possibility of faith, then we have no need of a reference to a single event in which that power is objectively overcome. And it is false to see only one alternative to the paradoxes of Paul and John, as if one could not speak of the power of sin and the opposing salvific and liberating act of God apart from a once-for-all exclusive event. For we have seen in

145

Matthew an example of a christology built upon different presuppositions. In the undercurrent of Matthew's thought, God's care, in whatever form it appears, is gracious activity in which humanity is blessed with the empowering command to love. My contention, then, is that a functional equivalent of the Pauline-Johannine union of indicative and imperative—when its reference to an exclusive act of God is discounted—is present in the Matthean gospel.

The significance of this contention is far-reaching. If it is correct, it means that there is a formal common denominator between Matthew on the one hand and Paul and John on the other /1/. The question, of course, is whether the substantive difference shown in the Pauline-Johannine reference to an exclusive act of God is of such character as to make illegitimate the interpretation of this theme in light of a notion of God's universal and continuing act of salvation, suggested by Matthew's undercurrent. We must ask, then, whether the messages of Paul and John are actually constituted by the christological paradoxes they proffer or whether one finds here, too, broader presuppositions which actually ground and sanction the confessional witnesses.

In the gospel of John, Jesus' statement that "no one comes to the father, but by me" (14:6) creates a genuine christological exclusivism. Salvation is explicitly limited to that effected through Jesus Christ. But in that Christ is identified (1:1ff.) with the Logos, through whom all creation itself comes into being, John's christological exclusivism is also a christological universalism. If Jesus as the incarnate Logos constitutes a unique act of God on behalf of human salvation, this unique act is nevertheless a historical manifestation of God's primordial saving act, present in creation itself. From the beginning, it is said, life was "in him" (1:4; see Brown: 26f.; Bultmann, 1971:44). And the primordial saving act is conceived as continuing, rather than punctiliar, since the Logos, as light, enlightens "every man" (1:9). It is only because, as Bultmann notes, the "Logos is constantly present as the light of men that the world can be σκοτία [darkness] at all. For darkness is neither a substance nor the sheer power of

fate; it is nothing other than the revolt against the light" (1971:47).
So John presupposes a kind of "natural revelation" which insures
the freedom and responsibility of human beings. Only on the basis
of the light they always have as God's creatures in the world do
they search for and perhaps find the authentic light when it
appears among them.

From a Whiteheadian perspective, the confessional lure toward
Jesus as the exclusive manifestation of the Logos opens into a
lure toward a recognition of the primordial Logos, already
present in experience per se. In a sense, then, it is once again the
universalistic lure that grounds and interprets the confessional
lure. So there is a real parallel between John and Matthew. But the
difference is that John, by explicitly proclaiming the exclusiveness
of the salvation Jesus brings, effectively unites the confessional
and universalistic lures. The universalistic lure is not allowed to
break through and show itself independently, since Jesus is
identified with the "true light that enlightens every man."

Now this union of christological and universalistic lures is, of
course, paradoxical. To the extent that it is claimed that only in
Jesus is salvation possible, the universal functioning of the Logos
is called into question. For if the primordial revelation is not
sufficient unto salvation, the question is to what extent it actually
insures human freedom and responsibility. Thus a
methodological problem of immense proportions arises.
Recognizing that a descriptive exegesis must accept the author's
paradoxical witness, for better or worse, what is the process
interpreter to say? May one appeal directly to Whitehead's dictum
that religious language is always in need of metaphysical
clarification (1927a:78) and thus put asunder, in the name of logic,
what the author has taken such pains to unite? Or could it not be
recognized—even from a Whiteheadian perspective—that the
author has a right to say something problematic? Perhaps, after
all, one must leave the paradox to the individual reader to deal
with in one way or another.

As far as I can see, there is no *a priori* way of answering this
question. But since John no more than Matthew exists in
isolation, its relevance for an appreciation of New Testament

christology as a whole cannot be determined apart from an examination of the other parts of that whole. And we can already see that Matthew is not utterly at odds with John on the issue at stake, since even for the latter christology in some sense serves a broader lure. There is thus some reason to think that the thought processes with which John is engaged would be served rather than aborted by a universalistic interpretation of the author's exclusivistic lure.

In the Pauline literature, we have an explicit reference to a primordial revelation (Rom 1-2), an "original possibility of authentic existence." But this reference is paradoxically used to show that creation is in fact shut up under sin. So the possibility of obedience indicated here is balanced by the inevitability of the misuse of this possibility. Nevertheless, it is of some significance that Paul—unlike John—overextends his paradoxical solution at 2:14: "When Gentiles who do not have the law do by nature what the law requires, they are a law unto themselves, even though they do not have the law." This clearly implies the reality of obedience to the divine command among pagans. And while this motif does not play as significant a role in Paul's thought as Matthew's extra-confessional lure does in his, it is an indication of the direction in which Paul's reflection upon the problem of christological exclusivism leads him. He cannot give an answer to the question he raises apart from a paradoxical formulation. But he is concerned enough with the problem of human freedom and responsibility that he implicitly violates his own solution.

Of equal significance is Paul's emphasis in Rom 4 on the faith of Abraham. Many interpreters have dealt with this phenomenon by reference to salvation-history or have argued that Abraham's faith is to be seen as proleptic faith in Jesus Christ. Boers has shown, however, that Paul treats this theme quite differently in Rom 4 than he does in Gal 3 (74-104). In the latter case, Paul speaks of Christ as the seed of Abraham, in whom the promise to Abraham is fulfilled. Christian faith is here related to Abraham's faith neither by virtue of the structure of faith itself, nor by virtue of the identify of faith's object (Jesus Christ) in both cases, but rather on the basis of the fact that through faith Christians participate in Christ, who is the "seed" in whom the promise is fulfilled: "for in Christ Jesus you are all sons of God, through faith" (Gal 3:26). Although Abraham's faith is not really proleptic faith in Jesus Christ, then, it is nevertheless related to Christian faith specifically because of Christ's role in the process of salvation. He stands as the "mediating point between Abraham and the peoples that are blessed in him (3:8; cf. 29)" (81) and, as such, the center of Paul's argument for justification by faith.

In Rom 4, however, the matter is fundamentally different. Here Paul proceeds from the assumption that Abraham, the father of Israel's faith, was justified in God's eyes. The question is how he was justified: Was it by works or by faith? Paul's answer is essentially a recounting of Abraham's experience in order to show that he was justified precisely through his persistence in believing, against all evidence to the contrary, that God would fulfill his promise. And in order to make this point he centers upon the nature, or structure, of faith itself: "Now to one who works, his wages are not reckoned as a gift but as his due. And to one who does not work but trusts him who justifies the ungodly, his faith is reckoned as righteousness" (Rom 4:4-5). "What Paul has to do," Boers argues,

> is to show that Abraham's faith was not a meritorious act, and that contrary to the Jewish understanding, Gen 15:6 was to be interpreted in this sense. He proceeds to do so, first by contrasting as a general principle a reckoning in accordance with what is due on the basis of works and a reckoning in accordance with grace where works are absent, and then, by applying this to the case of Abraham (verses 4f.). (87)

Paul's point is thus that Abraham's trusting *attitude* is a prototype of the *attitude* with which the Christian receives Jesus Christ as the agent of salvation. And in arguing this way, he clearly chooses to speak of faith in a generic sense. He interprets the nature of Christian faith by reference to a generalized faith in

God as the one who freely justifies the ungodly. Logically speaking, he implies that such faith is a possibility inherent in the human situation before God and that Jesus Christ is a servant of faith, and not vice-versa. Here it is not the figure of Christ—and certainly not the history of salvation—that connects the Christian's faith to Abraham's. Rather, as Boers notes, the point of contact is to be found in "the fact that it is the same God who is the object of the faith of Abraham (4:17; cf. 5) and of that of the Christian believer (verse 24)" (84). And this theistic emphasis is reinforced by I Cor 3:23, where Paul again betrays the ultimately subordinate role of his christology in relation to his consistent theism: ". . . and you are Christ's; and Christ is God's."

Now Paul's intention to witness specifically to Jesus Christ as God's unique act of salvation is undeniable, and the point of Rom 4 is finally to speak of faith in Christ. But the fact remains that in proceeding with his argument, both in Rom 1-2 and in Rom 4, Paul overextends his christological witness by giving place to an undercurrent quite similar to that in Matthew. In Paul, too, a theocentric emphasis encroaches upon the christology that is ostensibly the center of the text. Paul's "righteous gentiles" are such by virtue of their obedience to the Torah God has written upon their hearts; Abraham is righteous because of his trust in God's grace. So despite Paul's paradoxical answer to the question of human freedom and responsibility, there are indications that the negative or exclusivistic elements in his confessional lures are separable from the positive aspects—that, in other words, their ultimate role is to dramatize the positive truth-claim: in Jesus Christ, God freely gives salvation to humanity. If it is formally denied that God's universally given grace is elsewhere actually effective unto salvation, the denial is not necessary to the positive truth-claim and is even contradicted at those points where Paul's thought processes outrun his immediate intentions. At these points a universalistic lure reveals itself as the ground of the confessional by presenting a claim to a broader truth: God reveals himself in all times and places, so that his creatures may respond to him in trusting obedience.

A fundamentally different perspective is evident in Luke-Acts. Luke exhibits a concern for the question of human responsibility parallel to that seen in Rom 1-2. And Luke, like Paul, indicates that this revelation has been ignored. For the gentiles' worship, mentioned at Acts 17:23f., is a distortion of the intention of God's fixation of periods and boundaries of human habitation (vss. 26f.). And the present call to repentance is directed to "all men everywhere" (vs. 30). But vs. 30a shows how problematic Luke's solution to his own problem is. He cannot accept a fully paradoxical answer to the question of human freedom, so he proclaims the period before Christ the "times of ignorance," with the result that human responsibility in this period is in effect denied (cf. Acts 3:17). He thus sets himself at odds not only with Matthew but also with Paul and even John. For he does not maintain a distinction between a "possibility in principle" and "possibility in fact," but finally tends to deny even the theoretical possibility of the gentiles' knowledge of God before Christ. And yet this solution stands in tension with elements in his own argument: God did fix the boundaries of human habitation so that people "might feel after him and find him" (Acts 17:26). So even here we must speak of an undercurrent of anthropological thought which, from a Whiteheadian perspective, constitutes a universalistic lure. Although it is debatable to what extent such a lure is allowed to function meaningfully for Luke, we can say at least that it is present: he does appeal to human experience in general, although he (unlike Matthew) finally crushes that appeal under the weight of his system.

Hopefully, this selective overview will not appear tendentious. The major options in relating christology to soteriology are, I think, elucidated by this analysis. Even if it could be shown that at some other points in the New Testament the witness remains completely within the confessional realm, we would have to reckon with the fact that in each of the major works examined here a point of contact with Matthew's undercurrent was found. And that fact alone is perhaps enough to ground the assertion that Matthew's universalistic tendency is no mere aberration within the New Testament and so to legitimate a valuation of christology that does as much justice to that tendency as to the confessional dimension. But if we come at the problem from another angle and ask whether there is some way of discerning a normative layer of tradition by which to evaluate the various components of the New Testament on this question, the case becomes even stronger.

While I remain highly skeptical about the possibility of hard and fast knowledge of Jesus as a historical person, I cannot fully concur with Bultmann's designation of Jesus (1951-, Vol. 1:3ff.) as merely the "presupposition" of the New Testament. Willi Marxsen's perspective, I believe, leads to a much more acceptable statement of the case. Whether or not we are certain in attributing any given saying or theme to the actual historical person Jesus of Nazareth, the earliest proclamation *about* Jesus that stands behind the canonical texts would seem to have an obvious normative function in interpreting and evaluating the latter (64-128, especially 80f.; also Ogden: 1976). I refer here not to the earliest post-resurrection proclamation but to the implicitly kerygmatic pre-Easter tradition about his words and deeds. It is this earliest level of tradition, this apostolic witness, that constitutes a record of the initial impact of Jesus upon his followers, the impact that was in fact the genesis of the Christian message.

Because this apostolic witness to Jesus is itself implicitly kerygmatic or theologically motivated, the leap from this first level of tradition to the actual person of Jesus is problematic. But because it does constitute the earliest response to Jesus it nonetheless stands as the norm for all later theological formulations. If the inner life of Jesus remains inaccessible to scholarship, his impact upon his contemporaries does not. In uncovering this level of tradition we discover precisely how the "worlds" of those whom Jesus touched were actually reshaped. And if the inner lives of Jesus' original followers remain as inaccessible as his own life, the processes of "imaging" and conceptualization to which they were driven under his impact do not.

What we can discover, then, is the new self-*understanding* before God that emerged from their encounter with him. "The beginning," Marxsen says, "is not simply Jesus in his historical essence but in the direct apostolic witness to Jesus through faith" (81).

A reconstruction of the earliest tradition of Jesus' words and deeds is of obvious relevance to the present study. If an "implicit christology" can be attested at this level, one might argue with some force that the universalistic undercurrent to which I have pointed violates the norm by which the meaning of christological formulations must be determined. What, then, can be said about the portrait of Jesus that his original followers painted?

Dan Via's masterful study of the parables is particularly important in this connection, partly because it is in most respects compatible with the hermeneutical stance I have outlined. What is most significant is that he seeks explicitly to expose the fundamental ontological possibilities brought to expression in a parable:

> A parable as a whole dramatizes an ontological possibility—that which is there and possible in principle for man as man—and the two basic ontological (human) possibilities which the parables present are the gain or loss of existence, becoming authentic or inauthentic. The prodigal son gains his existence, and the unforgiving son loses his. But each parable also depicts how existence is ontically—actually and concretely—gained or lost, and the aesthetic form presses the two—the ontological and the ontic—into a unity. We could say then that each parable dramatizes how the basic human possibilities of gaining or losing existence may actually occur. (41)

Parables, then, "present their own autonomous world and make sense in themselves" (192). Thus one might fairly expect to hear that Jesus' message depends finally neither upon his self-reference nor upon an eschatological situation engendered by his presence. And Via does in fact say that the parables actually constitute "a demythologizing of" his announcement of the imminent Kingdom, "or, more correctly . . . a pre-mythological and aesthetic expression of the existential intention of the eschatology," so that they "indicate the eschatological crossing of the everyday" (186).

After all this, however, Via then joins the new hermeneutic in speaking of an "implicit christology" which grounds Jesus' call to decision in "a decision which he had made himself" (193). So the parables do not, after all, make full sense in themselves, but must be interpreted in light of the historic situation Jesus himself brings (191).

Now I can agree with Via that the parables point subsidiarily to Jesus' own ministry—to his acceptance of outsiders and his conflict with the religious authorities (192). But the question is what weight is to be assigned to this fact. It is one thing to say that the parables interpret Jesus' ministry and quite another to say that it is Jesus' own faith that is actually signified in his message, as Via implies when he says that "the coming of the kingdom is the possibility of faith's coming to man from beyond himself—as an act of God—and Jesus is the model for that faith" (193).

What one does with the evidence is a function of hermeneutical stance, and the approach presented in this study reveals an interlocking set of lures in the parables that demands a more complex explanation than Via has given. If a parable makes sense in itself, then it rests upon a presupposition regarding the fundamental nature of reality—that the universe is constructed in such a way as to justify the understanding of existence advocated in the parable. Thus the lure to imitate or reject any character in the parable also entails a correlative lure toward apprehension of the understanding of reality by which that character's life-style is judged. Such an understanding, although only implicit, is absolutely necessary to the signification the parable intends. If there is, on the other hand, also an implicit lure toward apprehension of Jesus' own deeds as exemplifying the principle in question (or, better, as another way of *announcing* that principle), it cannot logically be maintained that the apprehension of such a lure is functionally necessary. For it remains theoretically possible for one to grasp the significance of the parable to his or her own existence but miss the subsidiary reference to Jesus.

And if the implication that Jesus' actions exemplify the point of the parable—"that his behavior is God's deed" (Via, 192)—carries with it the implication that Jesus does represent the truth about human existence, it must nevertheless be said that there are two possible lures that may be identified in this formulation, one clearly more basic than the other. The basic lure is that toward a truth-judgment about Jesus' deeds as representing God's action; the correlative is that toward an understanding of God's action in Jesus' deeds as literally eschatological and exclusive. It is problematic to what extent the latter, correlative lure is really present at all in the parables—whether, in other words, Jesus actually claimed to "bring" the kingdom by his deeds or simply announced a kingdom already present (Boers: 25-56). But the question is, in any case, hardly determinative in the context of this analysis, for even if present this lure seems to serve the other: to the extent that one reflects upon Jesus' deeds in the context of the parables, it becomes necessary to pronounce a judgment on the question of whether those deeds are commensurate with God's will; it is not, however, necessary on the basis of the parables to complement this judgment with any particular conceptualization of Jesus' status—e.g., that he represents God in a literally eschatological or exclusive sense. On this reading, then, the primary function of Jesus' eschatological language is to dramatize the truth-claim inherent in his call to repentance.

Further confirmation of a universalistic element in Jesus' message is to be found in his wisdom sayings, such as the passages in the Sermon on the Mount treated in chapter 4 in terms of their Matthean setting. If these sayings, which presuppose a knowledge of God apart from a covenantal relationship and thus contain an appeal to reality as it is available to humanity generally, are taken seriously as elements in the earliest level of tradition, then the clear implication is that the new possibility Jesus presents is in fact a re-presentation of the primordial possibility.

Bultmann (1967) admits that this material presents a universalistic appeal, but argues that the "general truths" that form the basis of this appeal become effective proclamation only because they are concretized, through reference to Jesus' deeds, in the "now" of the person being addressed. Bultmann makes this judgment in light of the structure of the post-Easter message /2/, but there is a certain sense in which he is justified on the basis of Jesus' own eschatological emphasis. A general truth becomes an effective complement to the announcement of the Kingdom only if received as a word that God has spoken and not one that the hearer has merely "discovered." Otherwise it would weaken the claim that God is acting here and now. But once made, the appeal to a general truth nevertheless becomes the referent of the eschatological message and deeds. For the point of the appeal is this: if one could only see the truth inherent in experience per se, one could also discern in Jesus' deeds God's eschatological judgment. So what the wisdom sayings and the parables both show is that Jesus' eschatological word and deed presuppose a prior consciousness of God's activity. And if Jesus' message also presupposes that the people have largely suppressed that consciousness, the institutionalization of this suppression as a cosmic necessity is not an indispensable (or even particularly evident!) corollary of the claim that what Jesus says and does represents God to the people.

So the functioning of the universalistic lure would seem undeniable. And this discovery lends added weight to Van Harvey's contention that the study of the "historical Jesus"—contrary to the expectations of its proponents—actually helps Ogden to make his case (199f.). Jesus' message presupposes a revelation of God wholly apart from the factors injected by the imminence of the Kingdom and wholly apart from his own ministry—a revelation perfectly capable of fostering authentic existence. It is thus an announcement in the eschatological moment of just that obedience for which the people have always been responsible and of that forgiveness which God has always intended. Jesus' ministry may therefore be understood as the eschatological re-presentation of the "original possibility of authentic existence." As a sign of that radical grace and radical demand with which God now confronts the people, he has only to remind his hearers of the depth dimension of life as they and all human beings already know it: "Consider the lilies of the field. . . ."

Chapter 11

Interpreting the Christ-Image

The preceding venture into the wide range of New Testament christological formulations and the preaching of Jesus is, in my estimation, suggestive of a solution to the question under consideration in this study. With respect to Matthew, I have argued that it is legitimate to interpret his mainstream of thought in light of his undercurrent because the latter constitutes a universalistic lure that grounds and sanctions the confessional or particularistic lure toward Jesus as an object of faith. If I am accurate in claiming that Matthew's undercurrent is no mere aberration but is paralleled at other points in the New Testament—one of which is the logical norm for all later theological formulations—it would seem that this same judgment ought also to apply to the whole.

What, then, is the real nature of the New Testament's witness to Jesus as the Christ? It is, from the perspective of a process hermeneutic as I conceive it, a proximate lure which serves finally to point beyond itself bifocally: toward a particular human self-understanding on the one hand and toward an apprehension of God as the ultimate ground of this possibility on the other. A Whiteheadian analysis of the christological formulations of the New Testament leads the interpreter to look beyond the immediate discursive or doctrinal implications of the confession of Christ and to see it as an image or symbol which calls not for intellectual affirmation on a literal level but only for an existential commitment—but an existential commitment which carries with it implications regarding the fundamental structure of reality. The exclusivistic aspect of the Christ-image of the New Testament thus appears as a kind of *confessional hyperbole* that gives dramatic weight to the claim that is made /3/. And the image itself functions precisely as symbol, forfeiting its own self-reference in favor of the two foci toward which it points: God and the world of human beings.

It is of utmost importance to emphasize that the text's power to assert is by no means curtailed by such a reading. Whereas the exclusivistic dimension of the christological confession—when understood univocally, rather than as hyperbole—is an obstruction to the tacit universalistic reference, this broader reference grounds the entire confessional witness. The truth-judgment is a functional necessity at the level of basic assumption, for the legitimacy of the entire witness is undercut if one does not in fact believe in the reality toward which the text ultimately points.

The proximate christological lure, on the other hand, plays an indispensable role in the text's signification. One aspect of the truth-claim about Jesus does remain functional from the perspective proposed here. For precisely by deciding to trust in the God whom Jesus represents, the reader of the text necessarily implies a judgment about Jesus' revelatory function—or, to use the traditional theological term, his office. If the christological formulation is understood imagistically, however, this truth-judgment no longer includes a literal assent to its hyperbolic elements.

What emerges from a process analysis of the christological formulations of the New Testament is a christology beyond dogma—one that might aptly be termed a "paradigmatic" or "catalytic" christology. The New Testament focuses upon the image of Jesus as the Christ. It does so, however, not really in order to elicit a doctrinal affirmation about Jesus as the exclusive irruption of grace into human history, but rather ultimately to lure its readers into an encounter with that reality which comes to expression through him. Insofar as the call to Jesus as representing God's action actually presupposes God's universal activity, the Christ-image appears as a paradigm—as a sign of the way God always relates to his world. And insofar as the call to faith in a universally active God is conceived in terms of a proclamation of Jesus as the Christ, this Jesus is acknowledged as a kind of catalytic agent—i.e., as one who at a particular moment in history brings to full and definitive expression a possibility of existence before God always given in the human experience.

The New Testament, on this reading, points to Jesus as the one who re-presents God to the human community. In so doing, it thus acknowledges the actuality of human alienation, but does not institutionalize this alienation as a cosmic necessity. It presents Jesus as the one who shatters the alienated self-understanding by exposing precisely that genuine possibility which human beings have themselves corrupted. So the claim is neither that authentic existence is available purely and simply in human experience nor that Jesus creates a new possibility. It is, rather, that Jesus as the Christ catalyzes a possibility that God is always in the process of granting but which human beings generally distort. In the capacity of catalytic agent he thus *symbolizes,* for the Christian believer, what must always take place if authentic existence is actually to occur: life must be received, in trust, through some actual historical moment, as conveying a radical grace and a radical demand grounded in the core of reality itself. A paradigmatic or catalytic rendering of the Christ-image thus in no way neutralizes the Pauline-Johannine insistence upon the priority of grace /4/.

Chapter 12

Excursus

Quite obviously, my interpretation of New Testament christology stands in fundamental agreement with that of Schubert Ogden. So to the extent that my exegesis implies support for a systematic position also, it is important to attempt a clarification of a crucial point on which Ogden's view has been criticized. The question, in essence, is whether the notion of Jesus Christ as the re-presentation of the original possibility of authentic existence is really meaningful. For if the original possibility must be re-presented, are we not once again stuck with Bultmann's paradox? And does not the notion of re-presentaion, in any case, lead us into the problematic assertion that all human beings, in all times and places, have the same responsibilities before God, despite the radical differences in human cultures?

The first objection, I believe, may be answered rather easily. It is a commonplace of human experience that we obscure, through every ingenious device of psychological self-deception, what we do in one sense know, so that some kind of disruptive happening is "necessary" to bring us "to our senses." And our self-reproach at our own "forgetfulness" is proof positive that we have been "taught" by experience only what we knew all along, *on one level* of our thought processes, to be true /5/.

Moreover, Ogden's recent clarification regarding the "necessity" of christology is relevant here. While God's primordial revelation insures the possibility of *existential* realization of authentic existence in all moments in history, a special revelation is necessary for the "full and adequate understanding [of existence] at the level of explicit thought and speech" (1975:284). Thus the special revelation given in Jesus Christ is not *totally* redundant, since it adds something in terms of the possibilities for the conceptual objectification of the existential faith that is always and everywhere possible. But lest this formulation be taken as a shift away from Ogden's position as I have described it in chapter

161

3, it should be said that the kind of "necessity" here attributed to the Christ-event should in no way be associated with an "exclusivism of understanding." For to say that the Christian revelation is "necessary" in this sense is not to say that the particular historical event in which the Christian understanding had its genesis is the only event in all history—past, present, or future—which *could* mediate such an understanding. The necessity, in other words, lies with the understanding itself and not with the particularity of the event in which it did in fact emerge in human history. What Ogden is concerned to emphasize is that (assuming the truth of the Christian understanding of existence) the Christian revelation embodies a view of life that *objectively* represents the meaning of human existence, so that if a person is indeed to grasp in a reflective way what the meaning of life in fact is he or she must understand it precisely in the way represented by the Christian witness. But whether this *same* self-understanding is embodied in the reflection of some other group historically unrelated to the Christian movement remains a matter of phenomenological investigation rather than one of theological pronouncement /6/.

The second objection, regarding the non-historic character of a re-presentative (or catalytic) christology, is of peculiar importance in the present context, since it is frequently voiced from within the circle of process theologians. Thus David Griffin, in developing an alternative process christology, charges that

> Ogden seems to take [the primordial revelation of Romans 1-2] to mean that all are *equally* responsible for not actualizing authentic existence, since the primordial revelation of God already contained the content of the revelation in Jesus the Christ. This is, of course, the basis for Ogden's well-known rejection of the distinction between Christian existence as a possibility in principle for all men but a possibility in fact only for some. (1967:301)

While I can understand how such a conclusion could be drawn from some of Ogden's statements, I do not believe that it is really warranted. Nowhere does Ogden state that all human beings are equally responsible in a quantitative or material sense. All his argument on this matter actually entails is the assertion that all human beings in all times and places are responsible precisely at that ontological point of their constitution as human beings. He does not in any way deny that circumstance changes the degree of human freedom and thus alters the degree of responsibility for the realization of authentic existence. Nor does it follow from Ogden's arguments, or from my own, that the authentic existence for which the twentieth century Western Christian is responsible is exactly (materially) the same as that for which the Australian aborigine or the ancient Babylonian—or the Chistian in first-century Rome or modern Zimbabwe, for that matter—is responsible. It is perfectly compatible with Ogden's position to argue as follows. Time and circumstance *of course* change the mode of agapic response. But what they do not change—and it is this, I believe, that is entailed in the universalistic undercurrent in New Testament thought—is the formal character of authentic existence: it is always authentic to love one's neighbor, always authentic to approach life in an attitude of trust in the ultimate goodness of things, never authentic to act as if one's own small circle were the only creatures in existence, never authentic to view the universe as inimical to one's own being. But what it means, *concretely* to love, *concretely* to trust in the fundamental structure of the universe, is *of course* contingent upon historical circumstances. And *of course* the occurrence of some event in which the character of authentic existence is made fully explicit changes the degree of human responsibility /7/.

I believe, then, that a catalytic christology can in fact be developed in such a way as to preserve the historic character of the Christian faith, recognizing not only the paradigmatic function of the Christ-event but also the claim regarding the actual historical emergence, in the interaction between Jesus and his original followers, of the full consciousness of the human condition before God. But such a christology will preserve, nonetheless, the New Testament's insistence upon the basic, generic possibility given to humanity in God's primordial revelation—a possibility that is identical with the emergence of freedom and self-consciousness.

Chapter 13

Methodological Implications

In terms of the methodology of biblical interpretation, the net result of the present study is this: the use of a process understanding of the nature of the language of the text should free that text from doctrinalism so that it can be read as any other literary work ought to be read and hence enabled to do its work on both the imagistic and the conceptual levels. The text, as image, will appear less an answer than a question—i.e., an invitation to its readers to re-examine their lives in light of the symbol it conveys. And the question will not appear in the first instance as doctrinal, a matter of the literal truth of the content of the Christ-symbol. It will rather be existential, a matter of whether this symbol does in fact illumine life, whether it touches the readers at the level of their values and intentions. The real import, then, of the question, "Who do you say that I am?" lies in its function as a concrete way of asking, "Is that the way life is?"—i.e., of asking whether or not one sees that his or her existence is pervaded by the transcendent presence of the radical grace and radical demand the Christ-image conveys.

But the New Testament's question is not existential in a reductionist sense. For implied in the existential response to the image is a conceptual response also. To take a stance on "the way life is" is of course to make an implicit judgment about the universe in which one lives. If it is the image that questions one's existence, it is the lure toward an apprehension of reality as a whole that demands that the commitment embrace intellect as well as intentionality. So if interpretation is invited to engage the image in a free interplay that explores its intensely personal dimension, it is also asked to clarify the broadest presuppositions that ground that image and lay open to readers the implications of their attitudes toward it.

But to confront the conceptual question cannot, of course, mean to be asked to give a final answer to the meaning of the text—to uncover, once and for all, its ultimate reference and to state it in univocal fashion. Language is always an imperfect means of conveying meaning precisely because of the dynamic character of experience. Because a degree of abstraction from a complex and dynamic set of relationships is always involved in its genesis, no linguistic formulation ever fully expresses the propositions it seeks to indicate. Thus no discursive statement can ever replace the primal images in the text; interpretation will necessarily remain an ongoing interplay between image and conceptualization—but conceptualization based, of course, upon participation. So a Whiteheadian hermeneutic will be a *process* hermeneutic in the specific sense that it will always call for new encounters with the text and new attempts to allow its images to penetrate the present.

The catalytic rendering of the Christ-image presented in this study, for example, must be understood as based upon perceptions grounded in the peculiarly modern world-view—even though this interpretation, once made, actually becomes the basis of legitimation for further free interplay and reinterpretation. In a similar way, the very theistic reference that has appeared as the ground of the functioning of the Christ-image is itself subject to the same kind of critique I have carried out in relation to christology. One must determine what *kind* of a God is actually signified by asking which of the truth-claims regarding his being are dispensable proximate lures and which are necessary to the function of the witness of the text. Already one can see, on the basis of this study, the seeds of such a criticism in the Matthean gospel itself. Insofar as the reference to God is presented in conjunction with a univocal understanding of covenant thought, Torah-salvation, and christology, this reference too must be seen as containing hyperbolic elements in need of clarification in light of Matthew's undercurrent. What is important in this regard, I should think, is that God acts here and now, not that his action in any given instance is literally "unique," and that the obligation to the neighbor is grounded in the nature of human experience in the universe, not that it is the will of an external deity. To this extent I can agree with Ricoeur: "An idol must die so that a symbol of being may begin to speak" (467) /8/. *All* elements in the text, without exception, are subject to critique.

And this dynamic character of interpretation means that every new rendering becomes—for better or worse—a link in the ongoing process of *tradition* of which the text itself is a part. Thus the most creative interpreters will be those who are conscious of this fact and move beyond the illusion of pure description by allowing the life-and-death issues that belong to their places in history to open their eyes to the depth of the original author's thinking processes. To say that a text is freed to do its work, then, means that it is allowed to have its impact (both imagistically and conceptually) upon the aesthetic, ethical, social, political, and other dimensions of the consciousness of the reader—that it is freed for *unencumbered* dialogues with literature, politics, philosophy, and all other dimensions of the human experience. While ideological usage of the text is an ever-present danger, one misses the full thrust of the text if interpretation is limited to the restatement of its surface claims to doctrinal truth and ignores its potential impact upon present reality. Thus, for example, one can hardly claim fully to appreciate Matthew's judgment scene if a description of its christological and eschatological assertions is allowed to obscure the question of whether this image does not speak directly to the question of human liberation, in all its forms, in the context of the twentieth century.

Chapter 14

Summary

In conclusion, the christology of the New Testament appears, from the perspective of a process hermeneutic, as an image intended to engage the reader on an existential level with a particular feeling about life and to present this feeling as grounded in the depth of reality itself. If the hyperbolic elements in the image must be clarified by a critical analysis, the stumbling block that is inherent in the image remains. For if the Christ figure of the New Testament no longer appears as the exclusive irruption of grace into history, he nevertheless appears to those who are grasped by his words and deeds as the full and definitive disclosure of a grace always and forever being given in the universe. In this image they are surprised with a radical love which accepts them into an unbreakable fellowship with the ground of reality; in this image they are confronted with a radical call that bids them lay aside their selfish motives and find fulfillment in living for the sake of the total reality and broadest community in which they stand. In this image, too, they are faced with the question of how they can conceptualize the universe and the meaning of their lives within it. But it is finally the image, and not the conceptualization, that remains the controlling element. A process analysis does not reduce the word of the New Testament to a "meaning"; it rather exposes, all the more clearly, the objective of the witness: the *experience* of grace, the *act* of trust, the *deed* of mercy.

NOTES

/1/ My purpose is not to construct a systematic christology but to discover the underlying function of the christological witness in the New Testament. Finding a common denominator between Matthew and Paul says nothing as to the various ways in which one might conceptualize the relationship between grace and demand. I do not mean to imply, for example, that Paul's insistence on the priority of indicative over imperative should be replaced by Matthew's inclusion of the indicative within the giving of the imperative. What I do mean is that the exclusivistic form in which Paul states his indicative can legitimately be interpreted in light of the undercurrent he shares with Matthew and that such a rendering would not disrupt his pattern of grace/demand.

I do not, on the other hand, mean to equate Matthew's view with Paul's. In retaining the Law, Matthew clearly takes a different path from Paul. The fact that Law functions as grace does not by any means vitiate the fact that it is Law—obligation, demand—and that as such it retains the character of a rule imposed upon the human realm from without. To this extent Matthew's view is subject to Ricoeur's (442-54) criticism as belonging to the level of "religion" rather than "faith." But it should also be said that insofar as Matthew's universalistic lure toward the love-commandment transcends christological and covenantal thought it transcends Torah-salvation also. And insofar as it appears as "naturally" perceptible, as embedded in the human experience with life-in-the-world per se, rather than as an element in a supernaturally revealed set of laws, it achieves a truly existential character even as it claims cosmic grounding. So a process analysis reveals the seed of self-criticism in Matthew which opens the way for a "post-religious" reading of his witness in Ricoeur's sense.

/2/   "The address of the Christian proclamation, however, is something that a man cannot say to himself. He must always let it be said to him, for he cannot carry its truth with him as a possession" (157).

/3/   Cf. Tannehill (especially 11-37) who, from a quite different perspective, argues that much of the language of the New Testament must be understood as "forceful and imaginative" rhetoric which must not be reduced to discursive content but is designed to shock the reader, through its dramatic character, into soul-searching ruminations that question one's most fundamental values and presuppositions.

/4/   If a catalytic christology does not neutralize Paul's concept of grace neither does it impair the New Testament's witness to the event-character of revelation. Because a judgment about the truth Jesus brings entails a judgment about him as truth-bearer, the image of authentic existence that emerges from an encounter with him is necessarily an image of a possibility given by God to humanity always and only in a historical event. And this applies to the primordial revelation as well as to its re-presentation in Jesus Christ. What is assumed in the wisdom-sayings, for example, is not some kind of amorphous "general" revelation, but God's continuing *activity* through which he manifests care for the whole created order.

/5/   I discussed the ideas expressed here with Ogden in an interview in Dallas, Texas, June 8-9, 1967 and am convinced that they represent a valid extension of his own thoughts.

/6/   The material in this paragraph appeared in slightly different form in an earlier article in *Process Studies* (193, n. 2). A subsequent discussion with Ogden

(Dallas, Texas, January 12, 1977) leads me to believe that it accurately interprets his intentions.

/7/ If this interpretation of Ogden's view is correct, then some of the criticism directed at him from within the circle of process theologians regarding the "unhistoric" character of his christology would seem to be ill-founded. If there is in fact room within his perspective for the recognition of differences in the mode of realization of authentic existence, then even Cobb's suggestion (especially 203-220) regarding the possibility of further transformations of the Christian faith through encounter with other traditions will not necessarily be inimical to his view. But this is a complex question which requires much fuller treatment than I can give here. On one fundamental point, however, Ogden's approach stands in marked contrast to some of the alternative versions of process christology—the question of whether christology describes only the relationship between God and humanity disclosed in Jesus or also includes that between Jesus and God. Griffin, for example, is convinced that the latter theme is central to christology (cf., e.g., 1973:219ff.). So in order to preserve a sense of the speciality of God's act in Jesus, while avoiding a traditional supernaturalistic exclusivism, he argues that Jesus' historical context made possible God's provision of "initial aims" for Jesus' self-constitution which enabled him, by realizing those aims, to become God's supreme act of self-expression (1973:215-17). But for Ogden such speculation is unnecessary, since the point of christology is simply to speak of the human self-understanding before God that appears *through* the Chirst-event. If the present study skirts the issue posed by Griffin's view, it is because I am convinced that when the New Testament is read from the hermeneutical perspective herein proposed, Ogden's version of the "point" of christology is confirmed to the extent that the New Testament does not appear to *demand* the kind of statement Griffin seems to think it does. But whether a reflective understanding of New Testament christology *allows* elaboration along such lines or whether the content of the Christ-image is significantly illumined by such speculation is another question, and one that lies beyond the scope of this study. Thus although I have chosen a route quite different from Griffin's I do not suppose that my treatment has in any way "refuted" his christological formulations. As a matter of fact, I would argue that to the extent that Griffin also rejects traditional exclusivism, his approach, as well as Ogden's, actually depends upon a hermeneutical stance akin to that which I have outlined here.

/8/ Ricoeur would apparently consign all metaphysical attempts to the realm of idol-making. But if Whitehead's vision of language is correct, then the very texts we have examined demand not only an existential, but also a conceptual, response. And in that Whitehead's metaphysical scheme contains within it the principle of self-criticism and explicitly acknowledges the fragmentary character of (even metaphysical) language, I doubt that it is subject to the currently popular criticisms.

WORKS CONSULTED

Allen, W. C.
1907-1908   "The Keys of the Kingdom." *ET* 14:248-50.
Bacon, Benjamin W.
1930   *Studies in Matthew*. New York: Henry Holt and Company.
Barth, Gerhard
1963   "Matthew's Understanding of the Law." See Bornkamm: 58-164.
Bauer, J.B.
1955   "Das Milde Joch und die Ruhe, Mt. 11, 28-30." *ThZ* 17:99-106.
Bauer, Walter
1952   *A Greek-English Lexicon of the New Testament and Other Early Christian Literature*. Trans. and Eds. William F. Arndt and F. Wilbur Gingrich. Chicago: University of Chicago Press.
Betz, Hans Dieter
1967   "The Logion of the Easy Yoke and of Rest." *JBL* 86:10-24.
Blair, Edward P.
1960   *Jesus in the Gospel of Matthew*. Nashville: Abingdon Press.
Boers, Hendrikus
1971   *Theology out of the Ghetto: A New Testament Exegetical Study Concerning Religious Exclusiveness*. Leiden: E.J. Brill.
Bornkamm, Günther
1963   "End-Expectation and Church in Matthew." Pp. 15-51 in Gunther Bornkamm, Gerhard Barth, and Heinz Joachim Held, *Tradition and Interpretation in Matthew*. Trans. Percy Scott. Philadelphia: Westminster Press.
Braun, Herbert
1957   "Der Sinn der neutestamentlichen Theologie." *ZThK* 54:341-77.
Brown, Raymond E.
1966   *The Gospel According to John*. Vol. 1. Garden City, New York: Doubleday and Company.
Bultmann, Rudolf
1951-   *Theology of the New Testament*. Vols. 1 and 2. Trans. Kendrick Grobel. New York: Charles Scribner's Sons.
1958   *Jesus Christ and Mythology*. New York: Charles Scribner's Sons.
1961   "New Testament and Mythology." Pp. 1-44 in *Kerygma and Myth: A Theological Debate*. Ed. Hans Werner Bartsch and Trans. Reginald H. Fuller. New York: Harper and Row.
1963   *History of the Synoptic Tradition*. Trans. John Marsh. New York: Harper and Row.
1964a   *Glauben und Verstehen: Gesammelte Aufsätze von Rudolf Bultmann*. Vol. 1. Tübingen: J.C.B. Mohr.
1964b   "The Primitive Christian Kerygma and the Historical Jesus." Pp. 15-42 in *The Historical Jesus and the Kerygmatic Christ*. Eds. Carl E. Braaten and Roy A. Harrisville. Nashville: Abingdon Press.

1967   "General Truths and Christian Proclamation." Trans. Schubert M. Ogden. *JThCh* 4:153-62.

1971   *The Gospel of John: A Commentary.* Trans. G.R. Beasley-Murray, et. al. Philadelphia: Westminster Press.

Buri, Fritz

1952   "Entmythologisierung oder Engkerygmatisierung der Theologie." Pp. 85-101 in *Kerygma und Mythos: ein theologisches Gespräch.* Vol. 2. Ed. Hans Werner Bartsch. Hamburg: Reich und Heidrich.

Burton, Ernest DeWitt

1921   *A Critical and Exegetical Commentary on the Epistle to the Galatians.* Edinburgh: T. and T. Clark.

Cobb, John B., Jr.

1975   *Christ in a Pluralistic Age.* Philadelphia: Westminster.

Cope, Lamar

1969   "Matthew XXV:31-46 'The Sheep and the Goats' Reinterpreted." *NovT* 11:32-44.

Dalman, Gustaf

1902   *The Words of Jesus Considered in the Light of Post-Biblical Jewish Writings and the Aramaic Language.* Vol. 1. Trans. D.M. Kay. Edinburgh: T. and T. Clark.

Daube, David

1956   *The New Testament and Rabbinic Judaism.* London: The Althone Press.

Davies, W.D.

1953   "Knowledge in the Dead Sea Scrolls and Matthew 11:25-30." *HTR* 46:113-39.

1957   "Matthew 5, 17-48." In *Mélanges Bibliques: Rédigés en l'honneur de André Robert.* Paris: Bloud et Gay.

1964   *The Setting of the Sermon on the Mount.* Cambridge: Cambridge University Press.

Dodd, C. H.

1946   "Natural Law in the Bible." *Theology* 49:Part I, 130-33; Part II, 160-67.

1953   *New Testament Studies.* Manchester: Manchester University Press.

Dungan, David

1972   Review of H. Boers, *Theology out of the Ghetto. JAAR* 40:537-40

Ebeling, Gerhard

1966   *Theology and Proclamation: Dialogue with Bultmann.* Trans. John Riches. Philadelphia: Fortress Press.

Fenton, John Young

1963   "The Post-Liberal Christology of Christ Without Myth." *JR* 43:93-104.

Fuchs, Ernst

1960a   *Zur Frage nach dem historischen Jesus.* Tübingen: J.C.B. Mohr.

1960b   *Zum hermeneutischen Problem in der Theologie.* 2nd ed. Tübingen: J.C.B. Mohr.

Funk, Robert
1966   *Language, Hermeneutic, and Word of God: The Problem of Language in the New Testament.* New York: Harper and Row.
Furnish, Victor P.
1972   *The Love Command in the New Testament.* Nashville: Abingdon Press.
Gadamer, Hans-Georg
1965   *Wahrheit und Methode: Grundzüge einer philosophischen Hermeneutik.* Tübingen: J.C.B. Mohr.
Goedt, Michel de
1959   "L'explication de la parole de l'ivriae: Creation matthéene ou aboutissement d'une histoire littérairse?" *RB* 66:32-54.
Griffin, David
1967   "Schubert Ogden's Christology and the Possibilities of Process Philosophy." *CS* 50:290-303.
1973   *A Process Christology.* Philadelphia: Westminster Press.
Hahn, Ferdinand
1969   *The Titles of Jesus in Christology: Their History in Early Christianity.* Trans. Harold Knight and George Ogg. New York: World Publishing Company.
Harvey, Van A.
1966   *The Historian and the Believer: The Morality of Historical Knowledge and Christian Belief.* New York: The Macmillan Company.
Hasler, V.
1959   "Das Herzstück der Bergpredigt." *ThZ* 15:90-106.
Heidegger, Martin
1949   *Existence and Being.* Introduction and analysis by Werner Brock. London: Vision Press.
1962   *Being and Time.* Trans. John Macquarrie and Edward Robinson. New York: Harper and Row.
Honeymann, A.M.
1954-55   "Matthew V. 18 and the Validity of the Law." *NTS* 1:141-42.
Hummel, Reinhart
1966   *Die Auseinandersetzung zwischen Kirche und Judentum im Matthäusevangelium.* München: Kaiser Verlag.
Jeremias, Joachim
1963   *The Parables of Jesus.* Trans. S.H. Hooke. New York: Charles Scribner's Sons.
Johnson, Sherman E.
1951   "Matthew." Pp. 231-624 in *The Interpreter's Bible.* Ed. George A. Buttrick. Vol. 7. Nashville: Abingdon Press.
Käsemann, Ernest
1964   *Exegetische Versuche und Besinnungen.* Vol. 2. Göttingen: Vandenhoeck and Ruprecht.
Kierkegaard, Søren
1936   *Philosophical Fragments: Or A Fragment of Philosophy.* Princeton: Princeton University Press.

Kilpatrick, G.D.
1950 *The Origins of the Gospel According to St. Matthew.* Oxford: The Clarendon Press.

Kingsbury, Jack D.
1969 *The Parables of Jesus in Matthew 13: A Study in Redaction-Criticism.* Richmond: John Knox Press.
1975 *Matthew: Structure, Christology, Kingdom.* Philadelphia: Fortress Press.

Klostermann, Erich
1938 *Das Matthäusevangelium.* Tübingen: J.C.B. Mohr.

Krentz, Edgar
1964 "The Extent of Matthew's Prologue." *JBL* 83:409-14.

Kruijf, T. de
1962 *Der Sohn der lebendigen Gottes: Ein Beitrag zur Christologie des Matthäusevangelium.* Rome: E Pontifico Instituto Biblica.

Kürzinger, J.
1959 "Zur Komposition der Bergpredigt nach Matthäus." *Bib* 40:56-89.

Lambert, G.
1955 "Mon joug est aisé et mon fardeau leger." *NRT* 77:963-69.

Ljungman, Henrik
1954 *Das Gesetz Erfüllen. Mt 17ff und 3,15 untersucht.* Lund: C.W.K. Gleerup.

Lundeen, Lyman T.
1972 *Risk and Rhetoric in Religion: Whitehead's Theory of Language and the Discourse of Faith.* Philadelphia: Fortress Press.

Marxsen, Willi
1966 *The New Testament as the Church's Book.* Trans. James E. Mignard. Philadelphia: Fortress Press.

Merleau-Ponty, Maurice
1964 *Signs.* Trans. Richard C. McCleary. Evanston: Northwestern University Press.

Milton, Helen
1962 "The Structure of the Prologue in St. Matthew's Gospel." *JBL* 81:175-81.

Munck, Johannes
1959 *Paul and the Salvation of Mankind.* London: S.C.M. Press.

Oden, Thomas C.
1964 "The Alleged Structural Inconsistency in Bultmann." *JR* 44:193-200.

Ogden, Schubert M.
1960 "Introduction." Pp. 9-21 in Rudolf Bultmann, *Existence and Faith: Shorter Writings of Rudolf Bultmann.* Ed. and Trans. Schubert M. Ogden. New York: Meridian Books, Inc.
1961 *Christ Without Myth: A Study Based on the Theology of Rudolf Bultmann.* New York: Harper and Brothers.
1962 "The Significance of Rudolf Bultmann." *PSTJ* 15:17-27.
1966 *The Reality of God and Other Essays.* New York: Harper and Row.

1975   "The Point of Christology." *JR* 53:375-95.

1976   "The Authority of Scripture for Theology." *Int* 30:242-61.

1977   "Prolegomena to a Christian Theology of Nature." Pp. 125-36 in *A Rational Faith: Essays in Honor of Levi A. Olan.* Ed. Jack Bemporad. New York: KTAV Publishing House, Inc.

Perrin, Norman
1974   *The New Testament: An Introduction; Proclamation and Parenesis, Myth and History.* New York: Harcourt, Brace, Jovanovich.

Pregeant, Russell
1970   "Poetry and Abstraction: A Review of Robert Funk's *Language, Hermeneutic, and Word of God.*" *PSTJ* 23:18-25.

1976   "Matthew's 'Undercurrent' and Ogden's Christology." *PS* 6:181-94.

Quell, Gottfried, and Schrenk, Gottlob
1964   "δίκη, δίκαιος, δικαιοσύνη. . . ." Pp. 174-225 in *Theological Dictionary of the New Testament.* Vol. 2. Trans. and ed. Geoffrey W. Bromiley. Grand Rapids: Eerdmans.

Rad, Gerhard von
1965   *Old Testament Theology.* Vol. 2. Trans. D.M.G. Stalker. New York: Harper and Row.

Ramsey, Ian T.
1957   *Religious Language: An Empirical Placing of Theological Phrases.* New York: The Macmillan Company.

Ricoeur, Paul
1974   "Religion, Atheism, and Faith." Pp. 440-67 in Paul Ricoeur, *The Conflict of Interpretations.* Ed. Don Hide. Evanston: Northwestern University Press.

Robinson, James M.
1964   "Hermeneutic Since Barth." Pp. 1-77 in *The New Hermeneutic.* Eds. James M. Robinson and John B. Cobb, Jr. New York: Harper and Row.

1971   "Logoi Sophon: On the Gattung of Q." Pp. 71-113 in James M. Robinson and Helmut Koester, *Trajectories Through Early Christianity.* Philadelphia: Fortress Press.

Schlatter, Adolf
1963   *Der Evangelist Matthäus: Seine Sprache, sein Ziel, seine Selbständigkeit.* 6th ed. Stuttgart: Calwer Verlag.

Schniewind, Julius
1960   *Das Evangelium nach Matthäus.* Göttingen: Vandenhoeck und Ruprecht.

Schweizer, Eduard
1952   "Matth. 5, 17-20—Anmerkungen zum Gesetzverständnis des Matthäus. *ThL* 77:48-84.

Stendahl, Krister
1962   "Matthew." Pp. 769-98 in *Peake's Commentary on the Bible.* Eds. Matthew Black and H.H. Rowley. London: Thomas Nelson and Sons.

Strecker, Georg
1966   *Der Weg der Gerechtigkeit: Untersuchung zur Theologie des Matthäus.* Gottingen: Vandenhoeck und Ruprecht.
Suggs, M. Jack
1970   *Wisdom, Christology, and Law in Matthew's Gospel.* Cambridge, Massachusetts: Harvard University Press.
Tannehill, Robert C.
1975   *The Sword of His Mouth.* Philadelphia: Fortress Press; Missoula, Montana: Scholars Press.
Thompson, G.H.P.
1960   "Called—Proved—Obedient." *JTS* 11:1-12.
Trilling, Wolfgang
1964   *Das Wahre Israel: Studien zur Theologie des Matthäusevangeliums.* München: Kösel-Verlag.
Via, Dan O.
1967   *The Parables: Their Literary and Existential Dimension.* Philadelphia: Fortress Press.
Vögtle, Anton
1964   "Mt. 28, 16-20." Pp. 266-94 in *Texte und Untersuchungen zur Geschichte der altchristlichen Literatur* 87. Ed. F.L. Cross. Berlin: Akademie-Verlag.
Walker, William O.
1965-66   "Demythologizing and Christology." *RL* 35:67-80.
Whitehead, Alfred North
1927a   *Religion in the Making.* New York: The Macmillan Company.
1927b   *Symbolism: Its Meaning and Effect.* New York: The Macmillan Company.
1929   *Process and Reality: An Essay in Cosmology.* New York: The Macmillan Company.
1933   *Adventures of Ideas.* New York: The Macmillan Company.
1938   *Modes of Thought.* New York: The Macmillan Company.
Windisch, Hans
1928   "Die Sprüche vom Eingehen in das Reich Gottes." *ZNW* 27:163-92.
1951   *The Meaning of the Sermon on the Mount: A Contribution to the Historical Understanding of the Gospels and the Problem of their True Exegesis.* Philadelphia: Westminster Press.